Invest In Your Chil

Dear Parents,

Did you know that your children can lose up to 25 percent of their reading and math skills during summer vacation? Or that children whose schools incorporate project-based learning perform 26 percent better on standardized tests?

While children enjoy the summer break, they experience summer learning loss if they don't practice their skills. That is why we created Summer Vacation®—a fun, entertaining educational program to prevent summer learning loss.

The Summer Vacation Grade 4 Activity Book is packed with new, fun activities that will help your children succeed in school:

- New, teacher-approved activities that meet national curriculum standards
- All-new language and math exercises to prepare your child for the challenges of grade 4
- Fun science and world geography activities
- Motivating, skill-building activities that address a variety of learning styles
- New project section with activities that you and your child can complete together, including "Make a Working Volcano" and more
- Removable "volcano facts" charts

Although we've organized the book around daily lessons, your children can complete most of the exercises independently and work at the pace that's most comfortable for them.

Take a look at Grade 4's fun educational activities and see how Summer Vacation can help your children do their best.

What is summer learning loss?

If they do not practice, children lose, on average, more than two-and-a-half months of what they learned in the previous school year—mainly math skills. That's one day of schoolwork for every weekday of vacation.

Summer learning loss affects school year achievement

Studies have shown that the achievement gap between students with similar abilities is almost entirely due to summer learning loss. During the school year, students of different groups achieve at pretty much the same rate, but the summer months put students who don't practice at risk of falling behind. As each summer passes, they fall further and further behind their peers.

Preventing summer learning loss

While many of the causes for summer learning loss are well known, researchers believe that a fundamental cause is lack of educational materials in the home. The best solution is to keep a child learning over the summer through rich, motivating, and effective educational activities.

Sources:
Alexander, K.L., & Entwisle, D.R. (1996). "Schools and children at risk." A. Booth, & J.F. Dunn (Eds.). Family-school links: How do they affect educational outcomes? (pp. 67-89). Mahwah, NJ: Erlbaum.

Cooper, H., Charlton, K., Valentine, J. C., & Muhlenbruck, L. (2000). "Making the most of summer school: A meta-analytic and narrative review." Monographs of the Society for Research in Child Development, 65(1), 1-118. EJ 630 022.

Cooper, H., Nye, B., Charlton, K., Lindsay, J., & Greathouse, S. (1996). "The effects of summer vacation on achievement test scores: A narrative and meta-analytic review." Review of Educational Research, 66, 227-268.

Kerry, T. and Davies, B. (1998). "Summer learning loss: the evidence and a possible solution." Support for Learning, 13, 3, 118-22.

SUMMER VACATION®
TEACHER REVIEW PANEL

Our panel of distinguished educators was instrumental in ensuring that the Summer Vacation® program offers your child maximum educational benefit. This panel provided key ideas and feedback on all aspects of our workbook series. We welcome your feedback.

Cathy Cerveny, Baltimore, MD
Maryland Teacher of the Year, 1996
Fifth-grade teacher; Integrated
Language Arts curriculum writer
Served on Maryland's Professional
Standards and Teacher Education Board

Shulamit Raz, Los Gatos, CA
Diller Award for Excellence in
Jewish Education
Resource Teacher and Mentor Teacher
ESL teacher multi-grades
Kindergarten teacher

Laurie Sybert, Lake Ozark, MO
Missouri Teacher of the Year, 1999
Second-grade teacher
Elementary Science coordinator
Fulbright Teacher Scholar

Becky Miller, Mason, OH
Gifted Coordinator for Mason City Schools
Taught elementary grades 3 and 4
Adjunct Professor at
Xavier University

Melodie Rosenfeld, Pittsburgh, CA
2nd and 3rd grade teacher
State Model Magnet Program
Elementary Education Instructor
at a teacher's college

Gemma Hoskins, Bel Air, MD
Maryland Teacher of the Year, 1992
Technology Coordinator for school
Former fifth-grade teacher and
elementary teacher specialist

Charles Mercer, Washington, DC
District of Columbia Teacher of the Year,
1999 Worked at NASA's Education Program
Office Elementary Science
resource teacher, PK–6

Rita Bailey, Brantford, ON
Elementary School Principal
Former grade 1-8 teacher
Literacy Pilot Project School

Getting ready for FOURTH GRADE!

As a third grader, your child entered the world of abstract thinking and started making connections between reading and other classroom learning experiences to his or her own life experiences. Your third-grade graduate may be able to:

- write complex sentences, using more varied punctuation and capitalization.
- demonstrate good literal recall when reading to identify main idea, plot, characters and sequence.
- make inferences and predictions for story outcomes while reading.
- distinguish between fact and opinion.
- use reference materials, such as encyclopedias, atlases and dictionaries, as source material for writing.

- write paragraphs to include a topic sentence and main ideas supported by details.
- identify patterns, and establish and apply the pattern's rule.
- read a map, calendar or timeline to answer questions.
- find the perimeter of a given shape.
- compute multidigit addition and subtraction problems with regrouping.
- multiply numbers to 9×9, and solve related division facts.
- use standard and metric units.
- compare and order whole numbers.

Grade 4 Skills

In fourth grade, reading will become more important, as skills are applied to reading in the content areas. Students will be expected to practice reading, writing, listening, speaking and

**Richard Scott Griffin,
Mount Holly, NC**
North Carolina Teacher of the Year, 1996
Teaches grades 4-6—all subject areas
Served as Teacher Advisor to State
Board of Education

Rob O'Leary, Sidney, OH
School principal
Former fourth-grade teacher
Fellowship Award recipient from
Wright State University

Denise Johnson, New York, NY
Teacher Center Specialist in
Manhattan
Previously taught grades 4–8
Instructor at Brooklyn College

Jenlane Gee Matt, Modesto, CA
California Teacher of the Year, 1988
National Teacher of the Year
finalist, 1989
Third-grade teacher

Norma Jackson, Keller, TX
Texas Teacher of the Year, 1999
On special assignment as District Writing
Specialist for grades K–5
Second-grade teacher
Summer Activity Writing Specialist

Linda Ullah, Santa Clara, CA
Harold H. Hailer Award in
Instructional Technology
Former Special Education, Gifted and
Talented Education, Title 1 teacher
Technology and learning specialist
Teacher in Residence, Foothill College
Krause Center for Innovation

Vered Raz, New York, NY
Fine arts educator
Arts Education Research,
University Settlement
Former elementary school teacher

Carol Caverley, Acton, ON
Elementary School Principal
Course Instructor of Additional Qualifications
for Teachers: Literacy and Primary Education
Former Curriculum Program Consultant,
Junior Kindergarten to Grade 3

Please contact us at:
Attn: Summer Vacation, Entertainment Publications,
1414 E. Maple Road, Troy, Michigan 48083 or
e-mail us at: **summervacation@entertainment.com**.

Eveonne T. Lockhart, Cupertino, CA
Excellence in Education
Former 2nd and 3rd grade teacher
Middle School teacher

research skills in all areas of study. Your child, already proficient in basic math skills, will develop conceptual understanding and become a skillful problem solver. By the end of fourth grade, your child may be able to:

- identify and discuss parts of speech.
- read and discuss different writing genres (mystery, nonfiction, fantasy, myths, legends, autobiographies, historical fiction, and poetry).
- know how and when to use the dictionary, glossary and other resource materials.
- classify sentences as declarative (statements), interrogative (questions), exclamatory (exclamation), or commands.
- provide synonyms, antonyms and homonyms for given words.
- identify cause and effect.
- use context clues to decode unfamiliar vocabulary.
- recognize prefixes, suffixes and roots of English words.
- add and subtract fractions and decimals.

- identify patterns in multiplication and division sentences.
- multiply and divide by multidigit numbers.
- compute area and perimeter.
- explore percentages and their relationship to fractions and decimals.

How You Can Help

You can help prepare your child for fourth grade by making this Summer Vacation® workbook a regular part of your daily routine. Additionally, encourage your child to share the stories in this workbook. Get involved as your child constructs the volcano, and assist with additional research and completion of written activities. The Summer Vacation workbook is designed to help your child retain the skills that he or she developed in third grade and to prepare him or her for the challenges of fourth grade.

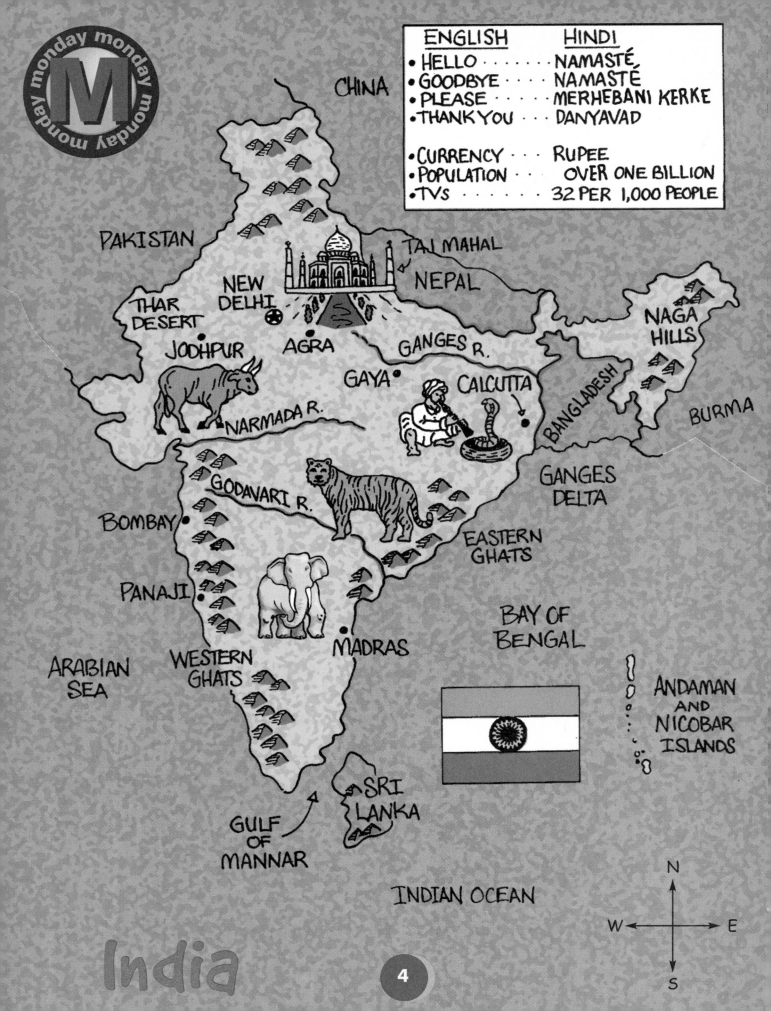

Crossword

INDIA

Across
1. Desert that borders Pakistan
2. River that runs south of Jodhpur
3. Eastern and Western _____
4. Island to the south

Down
1. Landmark
2. Hills in the eastern-most part of India
5. Endangered animal
6. Gulf between India and Sri Lanka
7. Eastern Bay
8. Sacred river

Facts About India

India is located in South Asia. The capital is New Delhi. India has numerous mountain ranges including the Himalayas, Eastern Ghats and Western Ghats. Located north of the sacred Ganges River is the Taj Mahal, a world famous landmark of India. The tiger, which is an endangered animal, is native to India.

Want to learn more about India? Visit http://www.interknowledge.com/india/

Addition and Subtraction Regrouping

Sometimes you need to regroup to solve addition and subtraction problems.

Examples

Examples

$$\begin{array}{r} {}^{7}8\!\!\!/3 \\ -56 \\ \hline 27 \end{array} \qquad \begin{array}{r} {}^{1}\ \\ 8\,7\!\!\!/4 \\ +19 \\ \hline 93 \end{array}$$

①
$$\begin{array}{r} 77 \\ -68 \\ \hline \end{array}$$

②
$$\begin{array}{r} 39 \\ +39 \\ \hline \end{array}$$

③
$$\begin{array}{r} 84 \\ -27 \\ \hline \end{array}$$

④
$$\begin{array}{r} 99 \\ +12 \\ \hline \end{array}$$

⑤
$$\begin{array}{r} 63 \\ -59 \\ \hline \end{array}$$

⑥
$$\begin{array}{r} 23 \\ +67 \\ \hline \end{array}$$

⑦
$$\begin{array}{r} 52 \\ -18 \\ \hline \end{array}$$

⑧
$$\begin{array}{r} 45 \\ +56 \\ \hline \end{array}$$

⑨
$$\begin{array}{r} 100 \\ -46 \\ \hline \end{array}$$

Math Riddles

Solve the problems below. Then write the letter on the bottom line that has the same number to solve the riddle. (Not all the letters will be used.)

(A)
576
+394
———

(D)
892
-418
———

(S)
4000
-3257
———

(L)
472
+281
———

(C)
582
+378
———

(E)
483
-226
———

(R)
948
-329
———

(P)
854
-266
———

(O)
626
+311
———

(F)
579
+326
———

(I)
538
+299
———

(K)
241
+685
———

What do Celeste, Vega and Tripp like to eat with peanut butter?

____ ____ ____ ____ ____ ____ ____
588   837   960   926   753   257   743

7

Journal

Use a blank sheet of paper if you need more space.

The leader of your country has asked you to help write some of the country's laws. If you could write three laws, what would they be? Why would these laws be important?

Sink Or Float?

Celeste, Vega and Tripp are testing their scientific knowledge by testing *buoyancy*. *Buoyancy* is the lifting force of water that allows some things to float while other things sink.

Test your knowledge of *buoyancy!* Complete the maze by correctly answering whether the object will sink or float.

Now do you own experiment! Form a *hypothesis* (or prediction) of what you think will happen in an experiment. What items in your house will sink in water? What items will float? Come up with a hypothesis by circling your guess in the "Hypthesis" column. Then test your *hypothesis* by conducting the experiment in a sink or a bucket of water. Fill out the chart below.

OBJECT	HYPOTHESIS	EXPERIMENT
	SINK/FLOAT	SINK/FLOAT
	SINK/FLOAT	SINK/FLOAT
	SINK/FLOAT	SINK/FLOAT
	SINK/FLOAT	SINK/FLOAT
	SINK/FLOAT	SINK/FLOAT
	SINK/FLOAT	SINK/FLOAT
	SINK/FLOAT	SINK/FLOAT
	SINK/FLOAT	SINK/FLOAT
	SINK/FLOAT	SINK/FLOAT

Matching Equations

Match the addition and multiplication problems that share the same answer.

1. 5 x 12   a. 10 x 5

2. 9 x 8   b. 12 + 60

3. 32 + 18   c. 17 + 43

4. 22 + 32   d. 9 x 6

Now match these addition and subtraction problems that share the same answer.

5. 72 − 14   a. 222 + 163

6. 115 − 87   b. 12 + 16

7. 400 − 36   c. 35 + 23

8. 509 − 124   d. 219 + 145

weird science

In a five-month span between 1987 and 1988, small pink frogs rained from the sky over parts of Great Britain!

Math Games

Do you see a pattern? Fill in the blanks with the correct number to complete the pattern.

1. (4) (7) (11) ( ) (22)

2. (12) (23) ( ) (48) (62)

3. (7) (10) (14) ( ) (25)

4. (17) ( ) (9) (5) (1)

5. ( ) (40) (32) (24) (16)

6. (21) (27) (33) ( ) (45)

Wanted: Volunteers

Chapter 1

Celeste, Vega and Tripp sat on the front stoop of Vega's apartment building. They ate ice cream cones while brainstorming ways to end their summer boredom. The three had been friends since Mrs. O'Leary's first grade, when they discovered that their favorite sandwich was peanut butter and pickles. Celeste, Vega and Tripp had had their share of fun. Tripp always found ways to carry out Vega's grand plans. Celeste, their artistic sidekick, helped bring beauty to each adventure. So it was unusual that after only one week of summer vacation, the trio had exhausted all that Springville had to offer for summer fun.

Vega, trying hard to slurp the fast drip of her ice cream cone, tossed out suggestions to Celeste and Tripp.

"We could play freeze tag in the fountain at the park," offered Vega.

"Keep still, Vega. How am I supposed to capture your good side?" Celeste said as she added the jaw line to the sketch she was making of Vega.

"What good side?" Tripp questioned with a grin. "Anyway," he said, "we did that yesterday."

"There's a new exhibit at the art museum that we could go to see," Celeste volunteered.

Celeste's suggestion was met by Tripp and Vega rolling their eyes.

During this discussion, the mail carrier came and handed Vega the mail. A bright orange flyer, folded and addressed to "Resident," caught Vega's attention.

As she scanned the flyer, her eyes grew wide with excitement.

Chapter 1

Skill: Nouns

Find these nouns from the story in the Word Search.

flyer   ice cream   sketch   carrier   friends

ideas   exhibit   tag   summer   pickles

I	C	E	C	R	E	A	M	N	T	E	F
Y	L	G	N	S	A	E	J	S	N	L	B
E	C	S	U	M	M	E	R	E	Y	I	R
P	X	T	E	O	P	N	M	E	C	O	A
O	E	H	D	R	L	M	R	R	S	U	D
P	F	R	I	E	N	D	S	K	K	C	G
S	I	S	R	B	L	O	I	D	E	A	S
I	S	C	S	A	I	O	A	T	T	R	O
C	D	C	K	O	N	T	U	L	C	R	E
L	E	S	H	L	Y	A	R	B	H	I	S
E	T	C	I	O	E	D	W	Q	R	E	U
W	I	K	N	E	P	S	M	O	W	R	D

Challenge

Some nouns are general. *Room*, *car* and *woman* are general nouns. Other nouns are more specific. They name a particular person, place, thing, or idea. For example, *sunroom*, *convertible* and *agent* are specific nouns. Writing that includes specific nouns is usually more interesting than writing that includes only general nouns. Write a specific noun that could replace each of the following general nouns.

1. shoe _____

2. tree _____

3. street _____

Fix the Facts

Sneaky Sal stole his sister Suzie's diary. He accidentally ripped out some of the pages and they fell out of order. Can you help Sal put the pages in order?

A.
I spoke with Mr. Juarez, my teacher, about Sal's idea. He said that a battery is a good idea and it will be a challenge for me to work on it.

B.
My brother Sal said that I shouldn't be making a volcano. He thinks I should make a battery instead. He's just my bratty brother. What does he know?

C.
I hate to admit it, but after talking with Mr. Juarez, I took Sal's advice and started making a battery. It actually works great and is the perfect project for the science fair. Maybe Sal is a lot smarter than I thought!

D.
My mom's helping me think of projects for the science fair. She said that a pizza box burglar alarm or a potato clock might be a good idea.

E.
I found out today that there's going to be a science fair at school. I really want to enter, but I don't know what to make!

F.
I started working on my project today. I didn't use my mom's idea, but came up with my own instead. A volcano! I'll need chicken wire, papier-mâché, paint, baking soda and vinegar.

1. _____   4. _____

2. _____   5. _____

3. _____   6. _____

Journal

Use a blank sheet of paper if you need more space.

I'm thankful today because...

_____

_____

_____

_____

_____

_____

_____

_____

_____

_____

_____

_____

_____

_____

_____

_____

_____

Crossword

ENGLAND

Across

1. Famous clock tower
2. Castle to the north
3. Major city in the southeast
5. Country to the west of Liverpool
6. Built over a river

Down

1. Channel by Stonehenge
4. Not the South Sea
7. Islands west of Ullapool

Facts about the United Kingdom

The United Kingdom is comprised of England, Scotland, Wales and Northern Ireland. The English Channel, the North Sea, the Irish Sea and the Atlantic Ocean surround the United Kingdom. In the southeast of England is London, the capital. London has many famous landmarks including the famous clock tower, Big Ben, and the Tower Bridge, built over the Thames River. Scotland has many beautiful castles including Inverary. Want to learn more about the castles in the United Kingdom? **Visit http://www.britainusa.org/4kids**

Add Up and Round Up!

Solve the addition problems.

① 465
   102
 + 30

② 542
   311
 + 32

③ 211
  87
 + 15

④ 178
  17
 + 6

⑤ 667
  39
 + 204

⑥ 316
  152
 + 77

Now, round each number to the nearest hundred. Use the number to create a bar graph below.

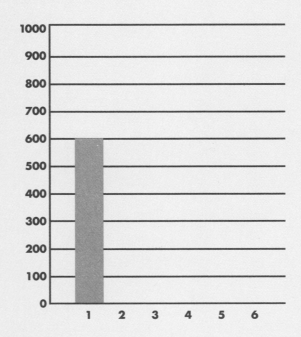

Lock Box Mystery!

Vega came up with another one of her grand schemes. She put away some of her money in four different boxes so that she wouldn't lose it. The only problem is that she doesn't remember the combination to the locks. Luckily, all of the locks follow the same pattern, and Celeste and Tripp wrote down some clues for the combinations. Use the clues to find the combinations for all four boxes.

The first box can be opened if you can solve these problems:

2 x 2   3 x 5   12 + 14   24 + 13

1. What is the combination? _____

2. What is the pattern? _____

Now that you know the pattern, use the pattern to figure out the other combinations.

3. 9, _____, _____, _____

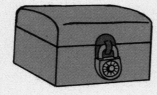

4. 13, _____, _____, _____

5. 6, _____, _____, _____

journal

Use a blank sheet of paper if you need more space.

Select three members of your family and describe them. How are they alike? How are they different?

Mix for Kicks

Celeste, Vega and Tripp decided to make some *mixtures* and *solutions* at home. They would take a glass of water and a spoonful of something to see if it would dissolve. If the material blended evenly in the water, like sugar, they made a *solution*. If the material mixed with the water but remained the same, like flour, they made a *mixture*.

Help Celeste, Vega and Tripp decide whether each item will be a solution or a mixture. Take the correct path in the maze to determine whether the items will make solutions or mixtures in water.

Now you can be the scientist! Create some *mixtures* and *solutions* in your own kitchen. First, get permission from an adult. Second, list items you want to test and come up with a

hypothesis. Then take a glass of water and a spoonful of an ingredient to see which ones will form *mixtures* and *solutions*. Fill out the chart below.

INGREDIENT	HYPOTHESIS	EXPERIMENT
	Mixture/Solution	Mixture/Solution
	Mixture/Solution	Mixture/Solution
	Mixture/Solution	Mixture/Solution
	Mixture/Solution	Mixture/Solution
	Mixture/Solution	Mixture/Solution

Place Value

Write the numbers in the correct places.

	Hundred Thousands	Ten Thousands	Thousands	Hundreds	Tens	Ones
1						
2						
3						
4						
5						
6						
7						

1. Six hundred eighty-two thousand, four hundred and five

2. Nine hundred ninety-six thousand, eight hundred and twenty-seven

3. Seventy thousand, five hundred and eleven

4. Three hundred thousand and fourteen

5. Three hundred four thousand, one hundred and twenty-two

6. Ninety-seven thousand and sixty-one

7. Five hundred thirty-two thousand, seven hundred and nine

weird science

Spinach is famous for having iron and making you strong. In fact, spinach has no more iron than any other vegetable. In the 1950s, a food scientist miscalculated the iron in spinach and put his decimal point too far to the right, making everyone think that spinach had ten times as much iron than it had.

Math Games

Each shape has a value. Scales 1 and 2 are in perfect balance.
How many triangles are needed on the right to balance scales 3, 4, 5, 6 and 7?

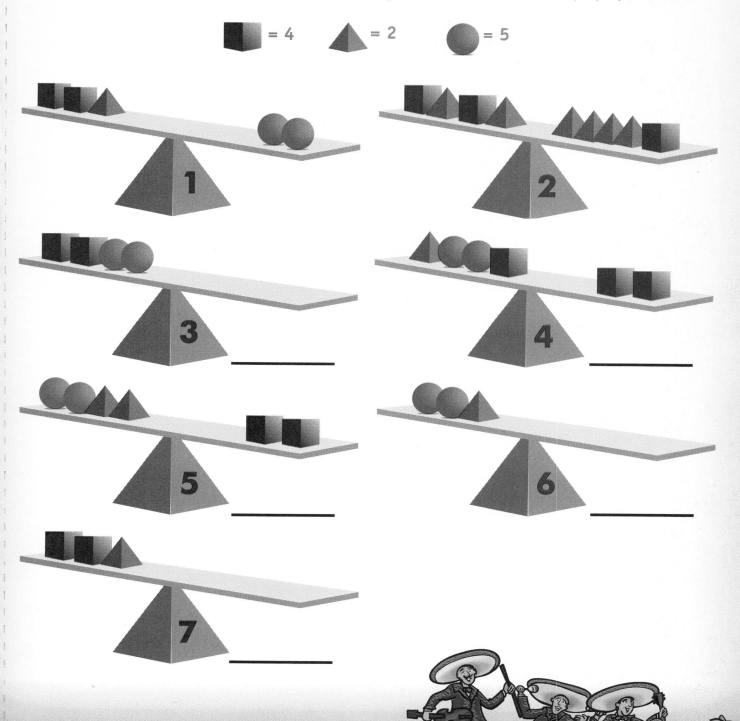

Wanted: Volunteers

Chapter 2

"Calling All Volunteers," read the first line of the brightly colored flyer.

Vega read the rest of the flyer aloud. "Springville Community Center challenges residents of all ages to bring their talents center stage and volunteer their time by creating and leading new summer programs. All serious proposals considered."

The mention of a challenge was enough to send Vega's mind into overdrive. Vega began to gently twirl a strand of her hair. Thoughts of how this challenge could be met filled every corner of her brain. Tripp and Celeste recognized this motion as the beginning of another of Vega's grand schemes.

"Guys, I know how we can help. All we have to do is..." started Vega.

"I know where this is going," interrupted Celeste. "Before you go any further, let me get my notebook and a pencil so we can start organizing your ideas."

Tripp was sure that this was going to bring much-needed excitement to their summer.

Celeste returned with a notebook and pencil. With heads together, the trio began sharing ideas of how they could help bring volunteers to the Community Center. They even talked about how they could volunteer. Finally, they decided they would help recruit community members to lead classes showcasing their cultural heritage with treasures or art. They went straight to work.

To start, Vega called and scheduled an appointment to present their proposal. Celeste began making posters to illustrate their plan. She used "It's Your Community Center. It's Up to You." as their slogan. Tripp organized a list of interesting people to recruit.

The friends were ready to present their ideas.

Chapter 2

Skill: Vocabulary

Choose the correct definition of each word from the story. Circle the letter in front of your choice.

1. **proposal**
   a. an officer
   b. stating something for consideration
   c. to display
   d. equal in size

2. **heritage**
   a. native dress
   b. an accent
   c. legacy, tradition
   d. country of birth

3. **illustrate**
   a. to follow a pattern
   b. to explain with drawings
   c. shining brightly
   d. to copy

4. **slogan**
   a. catchy phrase
   b. directions
   c. poster
   d. whispering

5. **trio**
   a. over and over again
   b. a large number
   c. silently
   d. a group of three

6. **cultural**
   a. helping plants and animals grow
   b. in a certain direction
   c. relating to the customs of a group
   d. relating to beauty

7. **recruit**
   a. to enlist new members
   b. to send
   c. to be quiet
   d. to be uncertain

Weird Verbs

Most of the time it's easy to put a verb in the past tense. Just add "ed" at the end.

Some weird verbs don't follow the rules, though. They have their own way of forming the past tense. Such verbs are called **irregular** verbs. Here are some examples:

Present	Past
Throw	Threw
Sell	Sold
Win	Won

Find The Weirdo Verbs!

To find the weirdo verbs, you have to figure out what they are first! Find the past tense of the following irregular verbs in the puzzle below. Words can be horizontal, vertical, diagonal or backwards.

Fly	_____	
Write	_____	
Eat	_____	
Read	_____	
Stand	_____	

Draw	_____	
Make	_____	
Sleep	_____	
Sing	_____	

S	A	D	E	N	C	W	E	L	F
P	L	R	O	D	Y	R	W	E	B
A	L	E	K	O	K	O	R	T	S
R	E	W	P	O	Q	T	U	A	U
E	N	F	A	T	U	E	N	Y	N
A	R	T	I	S	T	G	L	I	D
D	J	U	N	E	E	H	E	F	A
N	A	T	E	R	Y	L	A	R	E
O	I	L	R	I	G	E	D	A	M
A	M	Y	S	T	H	I	Z	L	U

28

OUT

IN

Compound Words

Mix up the compound words below and make up your own.
An example is done for you.

backyard   **nighttime**   **horseshoe**
moonlight   **butterfly**   **sunshine**
seashore   **bedroom**

___bedtime___   _____   _____

_____   _____   _____

Fishing for Synonyms

Synonyms are words that mean the same thing. Connect the fishermen with the fish that means the same as the word on their boats.

Journal

Use a blank sheet of paper if you need more space.

I'm thankful today because...

_____

_____

_____

_____

_____

_____

_____

_____

_____

_____

_____

_____

_____

_____

_____

_____

_____

_____

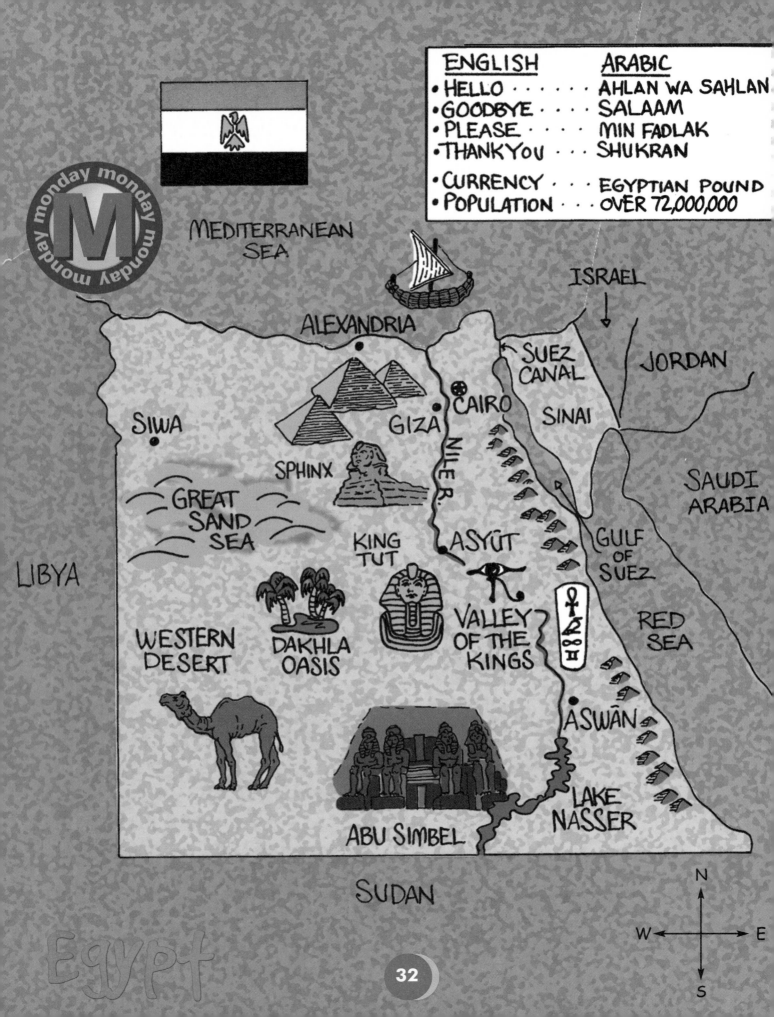

Crossword

EGYPT

Across
1. Northeast peninsula
2. Name of an oasis
3. Sea located on northern coast

Down
1. Country across the Red Sea
4. Country that borders to the west
5. Animals used for travel
6. Sea that borders to the east
7. Long river that runs through Egypt

Facts about Egypt

Egypt is located in the northeastern corner of Africa. Israel, Libya and Sudan border it. The Red Sea borders Egypt on the east near the Sinai Peninsula. The capital is Cairo. Famous landmarks in Egypt include the Nile River, which runs through Egypt, the pyramids, the Sphinx and the tomb of King Tut. Camels are used for travel in Egypt. Want to learn more about the pyramids of Egypt? **Visit http://www.nationalgeographic.com/pyramids/**

Fraction Comparisons

Write the fraction for each picture. Use < (less than), > (greater than), or = (equal to) to compare the fractions. The first one has been done for you.

1.

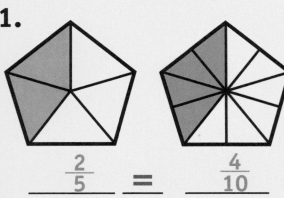

$$\frac{2}{5} = \frac{4}{10}$$

2.

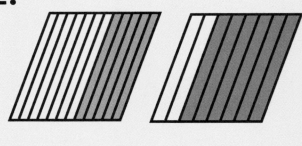

___ ___ ___

3.

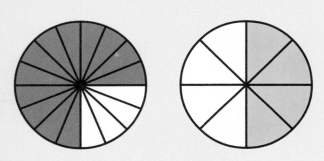

___ ___ ___

4.

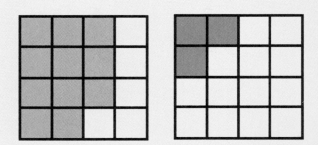

5.

___ ___ ___

6.

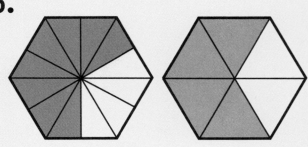

Pizza Party!

Celeste, Vega and Tripp love to eat pizza. Help them figure out what fraction each decimal is equal to by coloring the part of the pizza that equals the value of the decimal. Look at the picture to help you write down the fraction the pizza represents.

1. $0.4 = \dfrac{4}{10}$ **number of pieces left** / **total number of pieces**

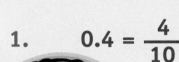

2. $0.8 = $ ____

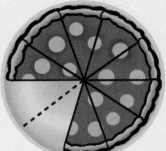

3. $0.5 = $ ____

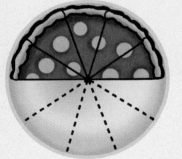

4. $0.6 = $ ____

5. $0.1 = $ ____

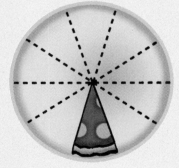

6. $0.2 = $ ____

Journal

Use a blank sheet of paper if you need more space.

Lucky you, you have just won the Megabucks Lottery! What will you do with all that money? Begin your story from the moment you receive the news and then explain how you will spend the money.

Home In The Biome!

During a visit to the local zoo, Celeste, Vega and Tripp noticed that the animals were not organized by their shape, color or size, but by the ecosystem they live in. A *biome* is a large area of land that includes both the physical environment and the things that live there. Earth has six major *biomes*.

Based on what you know about these six animals, decide which *biome* they most likely live in. To find your way through the maze, Choose from the two choices given on the maze.

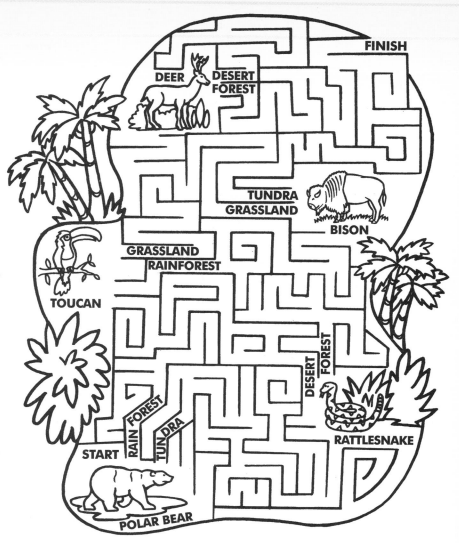

Biome	Characteristics
Tropical Rainforest	Warm temperatures and a lot of rainfall
Deciduous Forest	Changes in seasons, trees with leaves (oak & maples)
Grasslands	Light rainfall, tall grass but few trees
Desert	Hot temperatures during the day, very little water
Taiga	Long winters, trees with needle like leaves (evergreens)
Tundra	Low temperatures, layers of permanently frozen soil

Fractions As Decimals

Match the fraction to the equivalent decimal.

1. $\dfrac{6}{10}$

2. .8

3. $\dfrac{3}{10}$

4. .5

5. $\dfrac{2}{10}$

a. $\dfrac{8}{10}$

b. .3

c. $\dfrac{5}{10}$

d. .2

e. .6

Match these numbers in word form to the correct fraction or decimal.

6. one-fourth

7. seven-tenths

8. sixteen-hundredths

9. four-fifths

10. two-thirds

a. 0.16

b. $\dfrac{4}{5}$

c. $\dfrac{1}{4}$

d. 0.7

e. $\dfrac{2}{3}$

weird science

In 1964, an earthquake hit Prince William Sound in Alaska and was so strong that people in Hawaii could feel the aftershock!

Math Games

Do you see a pattern? Fill in the blanks with the correct number to complete the pattern.

1.

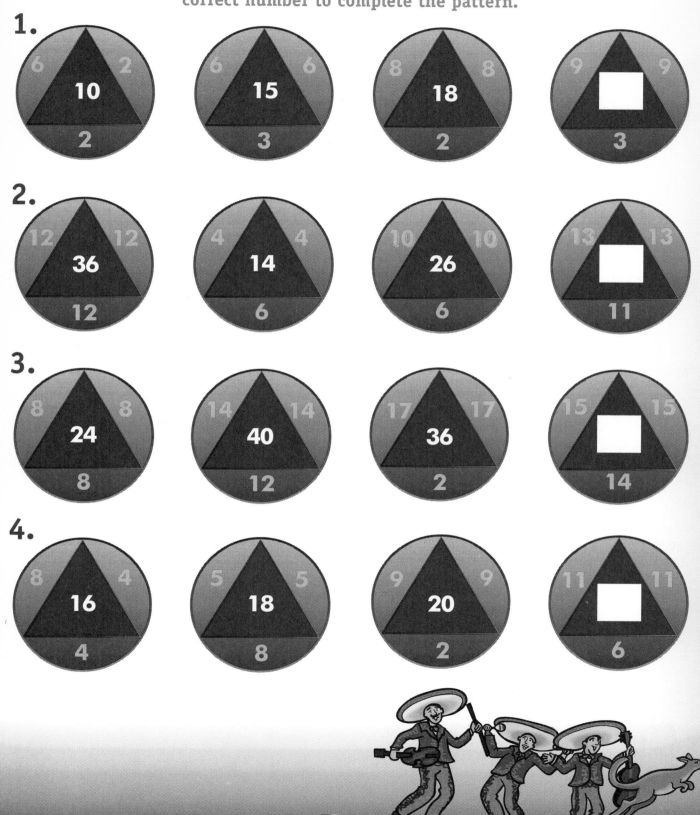

| | 6 / 2 / 10 / 2 | 6 / 6 / 15 / 3 | 8 / 8 / 18 / 2 | 9 / 9 / ☐ / 3 |

2. 12 / 12 / 36 / 12 — 4 / 4 / 14 / 6 — 10 / 10 / 26 / 6 — 13 / 13 / ☐ / 11

3. 8 / 8 / 24 / 8 — 14 / 14 / 40 / 12 — 17 / 17 / 36 / 2 — 15 / 15 / ☐ / 14

4. 8 / 4 / 16 / 4 — 5 / 5 / 18 / 8 — 9 / 9 / 20 / 2 — 11 / 11 / ☐ / 6

Wanted: Volunteers

Chapter 3

Celeste, Tripp and Vega nervously waited to meet with Pauline Darcy. Ms. Darcy had been the director of the Community Center for the last four years.

Looking very professional and wearing their Sunday best, they carried their posters into Ms. Darcy's office. Each took a turn describing a piece of their proposal.

"I would love to do all of your ideas," said Ms. Darcy with a smile. Tripp glowed. There was hope.

Ms. Darcy wasn't used to having people—much less nine-year-olds—in her office, throwing ideas at her. "The trouble is, the Center has barely enough funds as it is. Volunteers lead most activities that happen here, and they usually bring their own supplies. I'm afraid that we wouldn't have the money to get the materials needed for the volunteers to teach their classes." Tripp and the girls drooped.

Ms. Darcy knew it was hard news, but she didn't want to give the children false hope. "After last year's city budget cuts, I'm at the mercy of my volunteers to give not only their time but also their own supplies. This discourages many people from volunteering. They come to me with great ideas but don't have the money for supplies."

Tripp sat up straight. "What if we find a way to get volunteers and have them promise to bring their own materials?"

"If you can arrange that, I will take care of the rest," said Ms. Darcy.

Tripp thanked the director and almost pulled the girls out of the office.

"What's the big deal, Tripp?" Vega asked.

"You're not the only one with good ideas," Tripp said triumphantly.

Skill: Reading Comprehension

**Answer the questions below
on the lines provided.**

1. Where does the action in Chapter 3 take place?

_____

2. Who is Pauline Darcy?

_____

3. Were Ms. Darcy's answers angry or helpful?

_____

4. Who leads most of the activities at the Community Center?

_____

5. How have budget cuts affected activities at the Community Center?

_____

6. Why don't more people volunteer?

_____

7. What must happen in order for the children's plan to take place?

_____

8. Why is Tripp so excited at the end of the chapter?

_____

NOUNS YOU CAN'T SEE!

A noun is a word for a person, place, thing or idea. Words for things that you can see or touch are called *concrete nouns*, like house, teacher, and desk. Words for things that you cannot see or touch are called *abstract nouns*, like peace, happiness, and education. Some *abstract nouns* end in "ness," "ity," and "tion," like "sickness" or "hesitation."

NOUN SCAVENGER HUNT!

Let's go hunting for nouns! Read the newspaper article below. Circle all of the abstract nouns and underline all of the concrete nouns. The first few are done for you.

Community Center Offers Summer Classes

Due to budget cuts, the Springville Community Center will no longer receive money to hire instructors to teach summer classes. Center organizers say they will still offer summer classes and are asking for volunteers with skills to share to submit ideas for class subjects.

Volunteers should have knowledge, energy, time, and be able to provide things that will help the class learn, such as food, music, or photos. The Center has walls to display art and space for museum displays.

IN

OUT

Fun with Phonics

Sometimes two consonants together can make one letter sound. The "k" sound can be made by "ch," like in Christmas. Search for 10 words that use the letters "ch" to make the "k" sound.

B	A	G	W	C	H	O	C	S	U	I	O	M	N
H	N	C	I	H	S	T	C	H	O	R	U	S	C
E	A	C	H	N	G	X	S	I	R	Y	D	C	H
A	H	R	T	E	V	C	H	R	E	O	D	W	R
D	C	H	O	R	W	H	U	N	B	O	M	S	I
A	S	R	W	V	C	O	I	Z	A	H	G	E	S
C	T	C	H	E	D	R	M	P	C	T	R	Y	T
H	O	H	S	Q	O	D	R	J	K	H	R	Y	M
E	M	R	K	L	C	H	A	R	A	H	R	L	A
Z	A	I	H	B	H	U	W	M	C	H	L	O	S
O	C	C	H	O	R	F	S	M	H	U	R	F	L
C	H	R	Y	S	A	N	T	H	E	M	U	M	I

Cause and Effect

A cause is the reason for an event.
An effect is what happens as a result of a cause.
Match the proper causes and effects below.

Cause

1. I was starving,

2. My baby sister was sick,

3. There was lightning,

4. I have a big test tomorrow,

5. I fell off my bike,

6. My mom lost her key,

7. I was sick and had a fever,

8. I couldn't reach
the cabinet,

9. The power went out in
the house,

10. It was very windy outside,

Effect

a. so I am going to study
all night.

b. so they cancelled our
soccer game.

c. so she cried all night long.

d. so I ate two hamburgers.

e. so we had to call a locksmith.

f. so a tree branch fell in
my yard.

g. so I have a bruise on my arm.

h. so my dad gave me
some medicine.

i. so we got a flashlight.

j. so I went to get a chair
to stand on.

Journal

Use a blank sheet of paper if you need more space.

I'm thankful today because...

_____

_____

_____

_____

_____

_____

_____

_____

_____

_____

_____

_____

_____

_____

_____

_____

_____

_____

_____

CASTELLO DI AYMAVILLES

SWITZERLAND

AUSTRIA

MILAN

VENICE

GULF OF VENICE

FRANCE

PO RIVER

SAN REMO

PISA

FLORENCE

ADRIATIC SEA

LIGURIAN SEA

PESCARA

ROME

VATICAN CITY

MANFREDONIA

BRANDANO R.

NAPLES

CAPRI

GULF OF SALERNO

GULF OF TARANTO

CALABRIA

SICILY

IONIAN SEA

TEMPLE OF CONCORD

MEDITERRANEAN SEA

ENGLISH	ITALIAN
• HELLO	BUON GIORNO
• GOODBYE	ARRIVEDERCI
• PLEASE	PER FAVORE
• THANK YOU	GRAZIE
• CURRENCY	EURO
• POPULATION	OVER 57,000,000

Italy

N
W E
S

Crossword

ITALY

Across
1. This city is famous for gondolas
2. Sea to the east
3. Gulf south of Naples
4. Island south of Naples
5. Sea to the south of Calabria

Down
1. City (located near Rome)
2. Country that borders to the northeast
3. Southern island at the toe of the "boot"
6. Sea west of Pisa

Facts about Italy

Italy is located in South Central Europe. It occupies a peninsula that juts deep into the Mediterranean Sea. Italy is famous for its many beautiful cities such as Rome (the capital), Vatican City, Florence, Pisa, Milan and Venice with its gondolas. Ever wonder how Rome got its name? Learn this and other exciting facts about the Romans. **Visit http://www.bbc.co.uk/schools/romans/**

Matching Equations

Match the multiplication and division problems that share the same answer.

1. 96 ÷ 12

2. 6 x 6

3. 3 x 2

4. 100 ÷ 10

5. 8 x 5

6. 60 ÷ 2

7. 90 ÷ 10

8. 8 x 3

a. 36 ÷ 6

b. 80 ÷ 2

c. 48 ÷ 2

d. 3 x 3

e. 72 ÷ 2

f. 4 x 2

g. 5 x 2

h. 6 x 5

Mystery Picture

Celeste, Vega and Tripp are on a quest to find supplies for the Community Center. Solve the multiplication and division problems. When you are finished, find the answers in the boxes and shade those boxes.

1. 9 x 2 = _____   2. 6 x 4 = _____   3. 3 x 9 = _____

4. 7 x 6 = _____   5. 4 x 9 = _____   6. 56 ÷ 7 = _____

7. 5 x 8 = _____   8. 27 ÷ 9 = _____   9. 6 x 5 = _____

10. 54 ÷ 6 = _____   11. 7 x 7 = _____   12. 3 x 7 = _____

13. 2 x 6 = _____   14. 14 ÷ 7 = _____   15. 22 ÷ 2 = _____

16. 20 ÷ 4 = _____   17. 48 ÷ 8 = _____   18. 4 x 7 = _____

What did they find?

10	5	8	47	51	31	61	16	90	45
38	4	15	20	14	29	79	83	92	16
22	42	59	19	23	9	30	21	2	32
97	18	24	27	11	8	40	6	5	29
15	28	33	65	52	36	49	12	3	35
55	63	71	80	77	94	7	13	58	68
72	53	17	19	45	67	98	12	48	39

Journal

Use a blank sheet of paper if you need more space.

Have you ever been to the dentist's office? How did you feel? Can you imagine what your teeth might have been thinking? Write a story from the point of view of your teeth. Explain what happens to them and how they feel.

Manmade or Natural?

Celeste, Vega and Tripp have decided to create their own museum. They want to display *manmade* items in one exhibit and things made by nature in another. They've decided that a *natural* object is something found in nature that has not been changed or altered in any way. A *manmade* object is something that started out in nature but has been changed by people to become something new.

Help Celeste, Vega and Tripp decide where each item belongs by completing the maze below.

Create your own museum! Collect 5 items from your room that tell a lot about your personality and interests. List them below and then decide if they are *natural* or *manmade*.

1.	NATURAL/MANMADE
2.	NATURAL/MANMADE
3.	NATURAL/MANMADE
4.	NATURAL/MANMADE
5.	NATURAL/MANMADE

51

Comparing Numbers

Write the proper math symbol < (less than) or > (greater than) to compare the sets of numbers below.

1. 2,011,983 __ 2,102,871

2. 4,912,555 __ 4,976,555

3. 8,424,062 __ 8,423,062

4. 1,576,221 __ 1,621,999

5. 9,872,444 __ 8,872,444

6. 6,272,813 __ 6,222,813

7. 7,496,319 __ 7,948,324

8. 1,172,418 __ 1,127,426

9. 5,432,007 __ 5,007,432

weird science

The biggest spider in the world lives in South America and eats birds! They can have a leg span of more than 10 inches (25 cm) and weigh as much as 4 ounces (120 g).

Math Games

Do you see a pattern? Fill in the blanks with the correct number to complete the pattern.

1. 20   15   11   8   ___

2. 36   30   25   21   ___

3. 40   31   23   16   ___

4. 50   40   31   23   ___

5. 42   36   31   27   ___

6. 33   25   18   12   ___

Wanted: Volunteers

Chapter 4

Tripp added "SUPPLIES" to the bottom of his list of things to do. "First, we need to organize our list of people to recruit as volunteers."

Celeste knew this was going to be a challenge. "But whom do we recruit?"

"While you were making posters, I started a list of interesting people we know," answered Tripp.

Celeste and Vega added several more names to Tripp's list.

"Come with me," said Celeste suddenly. Tripp and Vega hurried to keep up with her. Soon, they were at the 8th Street Market.

The rhythm of a guitar, trumpet and violin belting out a salsa number stopped them in their tracks. They hardly noticed Mr. Gomez arranging a display of fresh vegetables.

"What can I do for you children today?"

Vega snapped her fingers. "Hey, this music is great." Celeste grinned and introduced her friends to the grocer, who was also her favorite uncle, Nick Gomez.

"How's your band, Uncle Nick?"

"Great!" said Mr. Gomez. "We play the next six weekends. Everybody needs music!"

"Oh," said Celeste sadly.

Mr. Gomez stopped with a handful of oranges. "What's the matter? This is good news…"

"Well," Celeste hesitated, "I was hoping that you could play at the Community Center—for free."

Mr. Gomez studied his oranges. Then he asked, "Can we do it on a weeknight?"

"You bet!" shouted Celeste as she hugged her uncle.

Tripp was puzzled. "What kind of band do you have, Mr. Gomez?"

Celeste pointed to a speaker in the ceiling. "That recording is of his mariachi band."

"Cool!" said Vega and Tripp together.

As the three left the market, Tripp was already thinking ahead. "Now all we need is food."

Skill: Sequence of Events

Number these events in the
order in which they occurred
in Chapter 4. Label the items
1 (first) through 8 (last).

_____ The children list people they want to recruit.

_____ Mr. Gomez agrees to play at the Community Center.

_____ Mr. Gomez talks about his band.

_____ Tripp reveals his plan for volunteering.

_____ Tripp starts thinking ahead.

_____ Vega notices the music.

_____ Celeste leads her friends to the 8th Street Market.

_____ Mr. Gomez is introduced as a character in the story.

CRAZY CAPERS

Who Drank the Last Can of Lemonade?

Jason's family is big. He has three sisters and two brothers, all of whom live together in one house with his parents and his grandfather, for a total of nine people. Can you help Jason figure out who drank the last can of lemonade? All of his sisters are allergic to lemons and his parents don't like lemonade, so the remaining suspects are his brothers, Christopher and Tony, and his grandfather. Listed at the bottom are important facts about Jason's suspects. Directly below are the clues Jason has to work with:

CLUES!!!

- When Jason ate a snack at 10:00 p.m. the night before, the can of lemonade was still in the refrigerator. The next morning it was gone.
- Christopher is younger than Jason and his bedtime is 9 p.m.
- At the dinner table the night the can was nabbed, Grandfather mentioned how salty and dry the food was.
- Tony left the house at 8:30 p.m. to go to the library. Jason was asleep when he came back.
- Jason found sticky spots on the first-floor patio the next morning.
- The patio's television was turned to the wacky science fiction channel, but the volume was turned down.

IMPORTANT FACTS!!!

- Grandfather lives in the attic and complains about his arthritis, which acts up at night and makes it impossible for him to move around.
- Tony is always studying and often drinks a lot of soda and juice to help stay awake. He also stays up very late at night.
- The can of lemonade was thrown in the garbage and had powdered sugar fingerprints on the side of it.
- Grandfather thinks science fiction is silly.
- Lemonade makes Christopher break out in hives. He also has posters of dinosaurs and the space rangers on his wall.
- Powdered sugar causes Tony's ankles to swell up so bad he can't put shoes on. He was barefoot the day after the can was swiped.

Who is It?!

IN → OUT →

Plural Endings

Plural means more than one. Sometimes words can be made plural by adding an "s," "es," or "ies." Sometimes the spelling of the word changes.

Write each word below with the correct plural spelling.

1. box _____

2. mouse _____

3. flower _____

4. leaf _____

5. tooth _____

6. beach _____

7. country _____

8. dish _____

Fishing for Antonyms

Antonyms are words that mean the opposite.
Match the fishermen with the fish that means the
opposite to the word on their boats.

Early

Huge

Dangerous

Black

Love

Nervous

Morning

Long

East

Late

Night

Short

White

Tiny

Hate

Relaxed

West

Safe

Journal

Use a blank sheet of paper if you need more space.

I'm thankful today because...

_____

_____

_____

_____

_____

_____

_____

_____

_____

_____

_____

_____

_____

_____

_____

_____

_____

Crossword

AUSTRALIA

Across

1. Animal known for hopping; females have pouches to hold their young
2. Famous structure in Sydney
4. City that lies between Sydney and Melbourne
6. Mountains found in the center
7. Cactus found here

Down

1. Type of marsupial found in this country
3. Sea found to the northeast
5. A reef off the northeast coast
8. Island to the south

Facts about Australia

Australia is the smallest continent and one of the largest countries in the world. It lies between the Pacific and Indian oceans. Canberra is the capital of Australia, located between Sydney and Melbourne. Kangaroos and koalas are marsupials found in Australia. People travel from all over the world to scuba dive near the Great Barrier Reef, which lies between the Coral Sea and the northwest part of Australia. Explore the wonders of the Great Barrier Reef. **Visit http://www.nationalgeographic.com/earthpulse/reef.** Take a tour of Australia's many museums. You can even create your own exhibit. **Visit http://www.amol.org.au/discovernet/**

Fraction Equations

Add or subtract the fractions as indicated.

① $\dfrac{1}{2} + \dfrac{1}{2} =$

② $\dfrac{7}{8} - \dfrac{5}{8} =$

③ $\dfrac{9}{10} + \dfrac{3}{10} =$

④ $\dfrac{6}{7} + \dfrac{5}{7} =$

⑤ $\dfrac{1}{6} + \dfrac{3}{6} =$

⑥ $\dfrac{3}{4} - \dfrac{2}{4} =$

⑦ $\dfrac{8}{9} + \dfrac{4}{9} =$

⑧ $\dfrac{5}{6} + \dfrac{1}{6} =$

Excellent Equivalents!

Celeste, Vega and Tripp have discovered that some fractions made with different numerators and denominators equal the same amount. Solve the following problems, then use the chart to list the equivalent fractions. In the chart, if two fractions end in the same place (like 3/6 and 4/8), they are equivalent. The first one is done for you.

1							
1/2				1/2			
1/3		1/3			1/3		
1/4		1/4		1/4		1/4	
1/5		1/5	1/5		1/5		1/5
1/6	1/6		1/6	1/6		1/6	1/6
1/8	1/8	1/8	1/8	1/8	1/8	1/8	1/8

1. 1/4 + 1/4 = __2/4__   Equivalent Fractions: __1/2, 3/6, 4/8__

2. 1/4 + 2/4 = _____   Equivalent Fractions: _____

3. 3/6 + 1/6 = _____   Equivalent Fractions: _____

4. 1/3 + 0/3 = _____   Equivalent Fractions: _____

5. 1/8 + 1/8 = _____   Equivalent Fractions: _____

Journal

Use a blank sheet of paper if you need more space.

What's your favorite meal? You have been asked by the publishers of a cookbook to describe this meal and explain why you like it. Use your five senses (touch, taste, smell, sight, and hearing) to describe what it's like to eat this meal.

Food!

Celeste, Vega and Tripp visited a grocery store and noticed that they were eating different parts of plants. Sometimes they would eat the *leaves* or the part of the plant that takes in sunlight. Another part is the *stem* that supports the plant and gives it shape. They also eat the *root*, which is the underground part that gives plants water and nutrients.

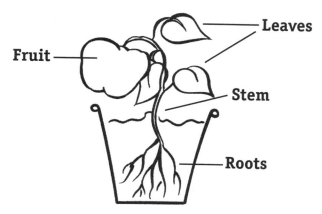

Help the kids decide what part of the plant they are eating. Circle the correct part from the options on the right.

	Celery	Leaves T	Stem E	Root A
	Carrot	Leaves R	Stem E	Root P
	Lettuce	Leaves R	Stem H	Root A
	Spinach	Leaves S	Stem N	Root U
	Radish	Leaves B	Stem P	Root O

Mystery Fact!

Each correct answer above is associated with a letter. Unscramble those letters to learn a mystery fact about plants!
Hint: I am a single germ from which flowerless plants like ferns and mushrooms grow.

____ ____ ____ ____ ____

Rounding

Round the following numbers to the nearest ten. If the number has five ones or more, round it up to the next highest ten. If it has four ones or less, round it down to the nearest ten.

Examples: 33 ➤ 30   55 ➤ 60

1. 78 ➤ _____   8. 37 ➤ _____

2. 14 ➤ _____   9. 16 ➤ _____

3. 22 ➤ _____   10. 43 ➤ _____

4. 66 ➤ _____   11. 57 ➤ _____

5. 62 ➤ _____   12. 81 ➤ _____

6. 47 ➤ _____   13. 85 ➤ _____

7. 54 ➤ _____   14. 73 ➤ _____

weird science

Some fish have luminescent (glow-in-the-dark) organs, like the Deep Sea Hatchet Fish!

Math Games

Each shape has a value. Scales 1 and 2 are in perfect balance.
How many circles are needed on the right to balance scales 3, 4, 5, 6, 7 and 8?

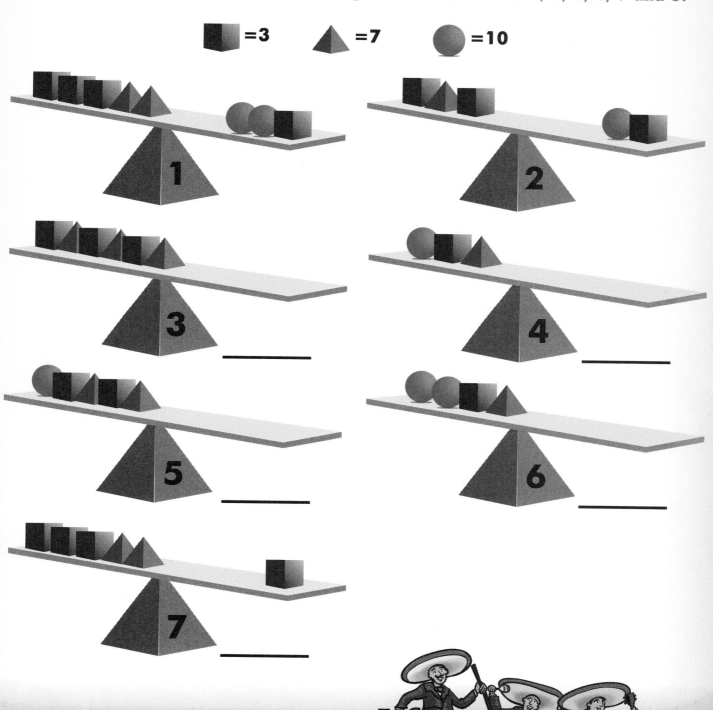

Wanted: Volunteers

Chapter 5

Celeste, Vega and Tripp got a late start the next day. As they entered the Athena Café for lunch, the delicious smells of grilled meat and vegetables made Tripp's mouth water. The café was a favorite spot, and almost everyone in the neighborhood knew the owner, Dmitri.

One of the children's favorite reasons for coming to the café was watching Dmitri prepare their food, especially *saganaki*. The flash of the Greek appetizer shooting fire as Dmitri lit the cheese always made them jump.

With their lunches on their plates, no one felt like talking. They just ate. The *gyros*, sandwiches made with pita bread, lamb, and grilled vegetables, disappeared quickly.

As they finished, Dmitri came over and slipped each of them a piece of *baklava*, a pastry with flaky, honey-sweet layers.

"Where did you learn to cook, Dmitri?" asked Celeste as she licked her fingers.

"What I know, I learned from my mother and from her mother," said Dmitri.

"Would you like to teach other people to cook?" asked Celeste.

Dmitri raised his eyebrows. "What are you kids up to?"

Vega laid out the plan. Dmitri could lead a cooking class at the Community Center.

"Well, kids," Dmitri began, "I have the café to run." He stared at the counter. Then he continued, "Something else my mother taught me was to go right to the source. Mother should be teaching your class. She's the expert."

"Would she do it?" asked Tripp.

"I think so," said Dmitri. "I'll ask her and let you know tomorrow."

Bursting with excitement, Tripp, Vega and Celeste thanked Dmitri and left the café. Vega reminded her friends about Thursday morning. "Come to my house at 9:30. See you then!"

Chapter 5

Skill: Determine Cause and Effect

Draw a line to connect each
cause with its effect.
The first one has been done for you.

Cause	Effect
Dmitri's mother and grandmother taught him to cook.	The children's food "disappeared."
The smells from the café kitchen were good.	Dmitri volunteers his mother to lead a cooking class.
Baklava has lots of honey in it.	Dmitri is a good cook.
Dmitri says that his mother is an expert cook.	Dmitri cannot volunteer at the Center.
The children ate their lunches.	Tripp's mouth watered.
Dmitri has to run his café.	Celeste has to lick her fingers.

Fix the Facts

Mr. and Mrs. McCarthy are planning a trip to Hawaii. Their two children, Blythe and Jack, will be going with them. They planned their trip over a couple of days. Can you put their conversations in order?

A.
"The islands are so beautiful. I can't wait to really see them. Can we see a volcano? Can we swim in the ocean, Mom?"

B.
"I called the travel agent just like I said I would last night. He set up a great deal for us: sightseeing, a nice hotel on the ocean, meals and Hawaiian luaus will be a part of the package."

C.
"Let's decide what islands we want to see first, children. Then we can decide what we want to do when we get there. We need to decide on an airline and hotel also. I wonder if any travel packages would appeal to us?"

D.
"I will call the travel agency in the morning and see if they have any packages available. I will ask if they have specific packages for families that include seeing a volcano."

E.
"Good morning, Mr. Turner. I'm interested in a trip to Hawaii. Do you have any packages available that would be nice for a family of four?"

F.
"We will be leaving at 8:00 a.m., May 30th. We'll have to get up early, so we should be completely packed the night before. It takes an hour to get to the airport, so we should be out the door by 6:00 a.m. Then it's HELLO HAWAII!"

1. _____   4. _____

2. _____   5. _____

3. _____   6. _____

OUT ⬋ ⬊ IN

Possessive Nouns

Possessive nouns tell who or what is the owner of something.
Singular possessive nouns take an apostrophe before the "s."
Example: The lion has cubs. lion's cubs
Plural possessive nouns take an apostrophe after the "s."
Example: The lions have cubs. lions' cubs

Rewrite each noun as singular or plural possessive.

1. sailors ships _____

2. waiter tip _____

3. teacher chalkboard _____

4. kids toys _____

5. lifeguards stations _____

6. actors costumes _____

Past Tense Verbs

Change each verb below to the past tense.
Then write a sentence using that past tense verb.
A past tense verb tells about something that already happened.

1. stop   stopped – My uncle stopped the car.

2. blow   _____

3. tell   _____

4. sing   _____

5. cook   _____

6. watch   _____

7. run   _____

8. grow   _____

9. come   _____

10. drive   _____

11. eat   _____

12. take   _____

13. throw   _____

14. make   _____

15. give   _____

Journal

Use a blank sheet of paper if you need more space.

I'm thankful today because...

_____

_____

_____

_____

_____

_____

_____

_____

_____

_____

_____

_____

_____

_____

_____

_____

_____

_____

_____

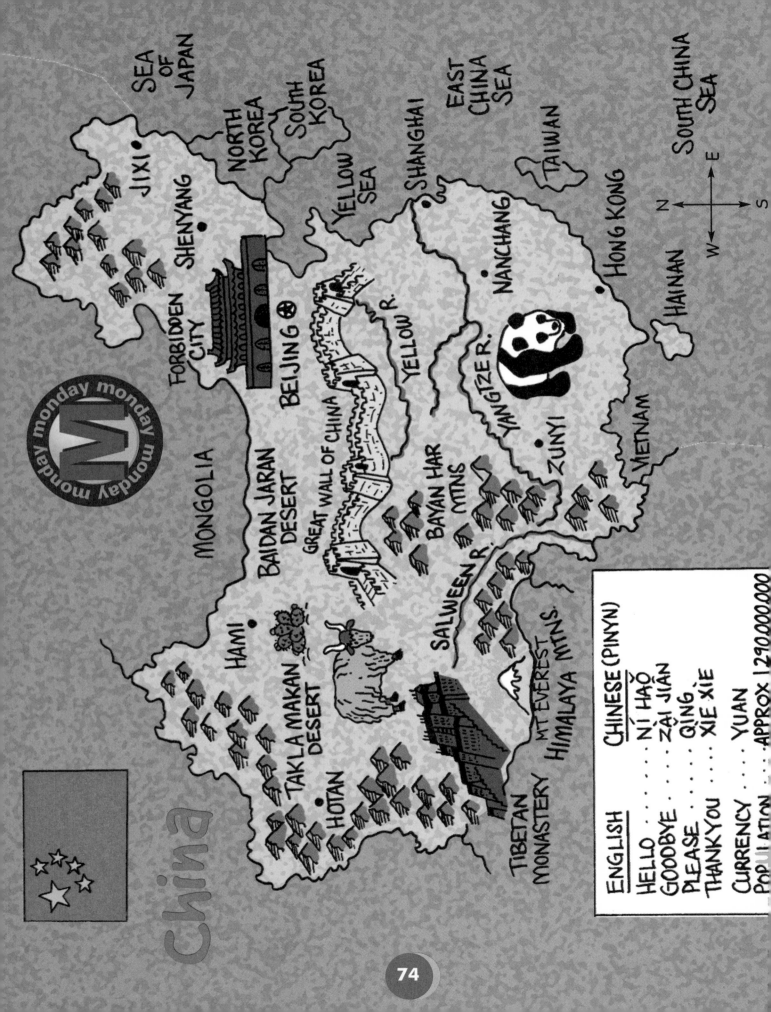

Crossword

CHINA

Across

1. This monastery is located in the southwest corner
2. These mountains are located in the Southwest
3. This sea lies between China and the Koreas
4. Popular animal
5. Tallest mountain in the world on the southwest border

Down

1. This island lies off the southeast coast
3. This river runs across half of China
6. This island is south of Hong Kong
7. This landmark is found in the capital
8. This landmark was built to protect China

Facts about China

China is the largest of all Asian countries and has the largest population of any country in the world. Beijing is the capital and the home of the Forbidden City. Other famous landmarks include the Tibetan Monastery, the Great Wall and Mt. Everest, the tallest mountain in the world. Panda bears are native to China.

Learn all about the Giant Panda. Watch a video and see a map of where they live.
Visit http://www.nationalgeographic.com/kids/creature_feature/0011/pandas.html

Multiplication and Division

Complete the equations below.

①
$$\begin{array}{r} 9 \\ \times\ 8 \\ \hline \end{array}$$

② $11\overline{\smash{)}99}$

③
$$\begin{array}{r} 12 \\ \times\ 3 \\ \hline \end{array}$$

④ $6\overline{\smash{)}36}$

⑤
$$\begin{array}{r} 10 \\ \times\ 10 \\ \hline \end{array}$$

⑦ $9\overline{\smash{)}81}$

⑧
$$\begin{array}{r} 5 \\ \times\ 9 \\ \hline \end{array}$$

⑥ $8\overline{\smash{)}64}$

76

Search and Seek!

Solve the problems below. Connect the red dot next to your answer to the red dot next to the same number in word form. Write the letter to the right of that word on the line at the bottom of the page above the same number. The first one has been done for you.

1. 7 x 7 = _49_ •   • eight   **E**

2. 56 ÷ 7 = _____ •   • twenty-four   **S**

3. 3 x 8 = _____ •   • twenty-eight   **T**

4. 7 x 6 = _____ •   • forty-nine   **U**

5. 54 ÷ 9 = _____ •   • eighteen   **L**

6. 40 ÷ 8 = _____ •   • six   **R**

7. 3 x 6 = _____ •   • four   **O**

8. 7 x 4 = _____ •   • forty-two   **N**

9. 32 ÷ 8 = _____ •   • five   **E**

10. 18 ÷ 2 = _____ •   • nine   **V**

What are Celeste, Vega and Tripp looking for?

____ ____ ____ _U__ ____ ____ ____ ____ ____ ____
 9   4   18   49   42   28   5   8   6   24

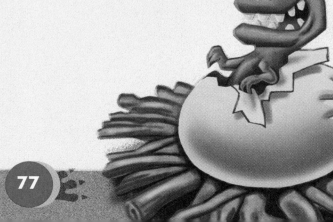

Journal

Use a blank sheet of paper if you need more space.

It's summer vacation, and you feel that you should have a much later bedtime. Write a letter to your parents explaining what your new bedtime should be and why this is a good idea.

Food Groups

Celeste, Vega and Tripp have learned about the food pyramid and the foods that belong in each group. Using the pyramid below, help them figure out what foods they are eating.

Circle the food groups that can be found in each item. Use the letters under each answer you circled to unscramble and solve the riddle below.

(The first one has been done for you.)

Cheese Pizza	Vegetable E	Bread & Cereal P	Meat B	Fruit S	Milk O
Turkey Sandwich	Vegetable A	Bread & Cereal P	Meat E	Fruit H	Milk R
Bowl of Cereal with Milk	Vegetable O	Bread & Cereal P	Meat A	Fruit U	Milk N
Yogurt with Strawberries	Vegetable A	Bread & Cereal C	Meat S	Fruit R	Milk I

Guess Who I Am!

I am America's favorite pizza topping. What am I?

_____ _____ _____ _____ _____ _____ _____ _____ _____

Story Problems

1. Your family is planning a trip to China. Round trip airline tickets will cost $900.00 each and there are four of you going on the trip. You will also need to bring $2,000.00 for spending money. How much money will this trip cost?

_____

2. You will be staying in a hotel that charges $200.00 per night. Your family will be staying there for six nights. How much will the hotel stay cost?

_____

3. Using your answers for problems 1 and 2, what is your new total for the cost of this trip to China?

_____

weird science

A fellow named Galileo was the first to discover the moons of Jupiter. He did it with a telescope that was about as strong as a pair of ordinary binoculars!

Math Games

Do you see a pattern? Fill in the blanks with the correct number to complete the pattern.

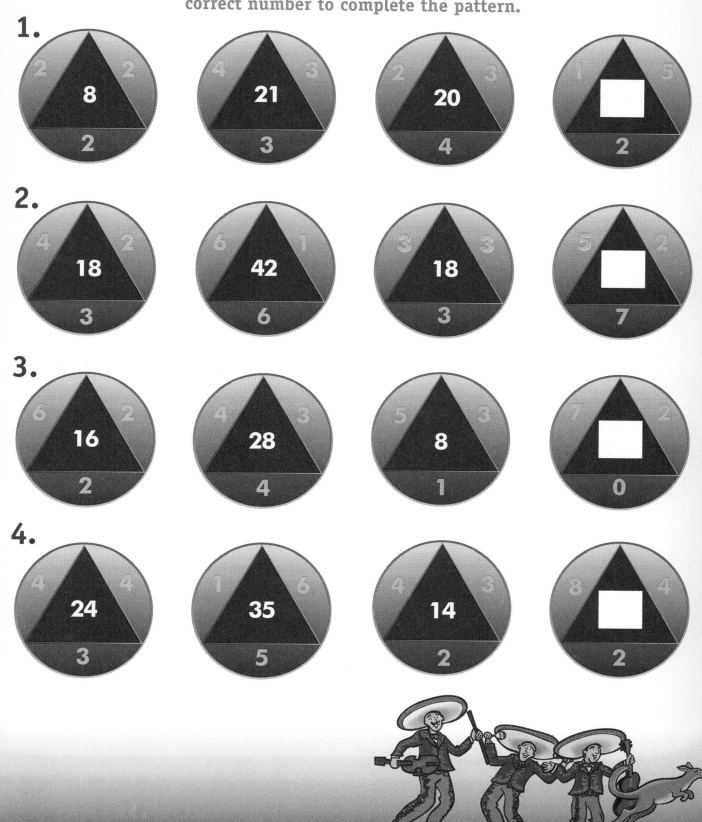

Wanted: Volunteers

Chapter 6

The three friends met at Vega's house the next morning. Vega hoped to recruit her neighbor, Mrs. Radanovich, as a volunteer.

Vega loved visiting Mrs. Radanovich and seeing the treasures in her house. Family photos lined a hallway, handwoven linen lined shelves, and a painted Fabergé egg held a secret treasure inside.

Mrs. Radanovich told stories about her childhood in Russia. "I was eleven. I came here with my parents. My older sister stayed behind with her new husband. It was a terrible and exciting time."

Tripp noticed the sadness in her eyes and in her voice.

"I haven't seen my sister since. Money has been tight, and she has not been able to visit."

Vega couldn't wait. "Mrs. Radanovich, would you please show my friends your collection?"

Mrs. Radanovich led them into a room where every shelf was lined with wooden dolls. There were several versions of each doll, each one smaller than the next. "The smallest one is no bigger than a thimble," she said. "I gave that to my sister to remember me by."

"They're beautiful," said Celeste.

"They're *matryushka* dolls," explained Mrs. Radanovich. "They're made from a single block of wood. Each doll opens to hold the next smaller size."

"Mrs. Radanovich, would you share your dolls with people at the Community Center?" Vega asked.

"Oh, I'm a little old to be showing off my doll collection," said Mrs. Radanovich.

"People would love to learn how they're made," Vega added.

Mrs. Radanovich gave in. Vega was sure that even the *matryushka* dolls smiled.

Outside, the three children parted ways. Celeste went to work on the mural she was painting for the Center. Vega stayed to help Mrs. Radanovich. Tripp, acting secretive, said he had an errand to run.

Chapter 6

Skill: Verbs

Connect the verbs to help Vega, Tripp and Celeste get to the Community Center. The path goes up, down, and sideways, but not diagonally. When you have finished, use each verb you have found in a sentence. Write your sentences on a separate sheet of paper.

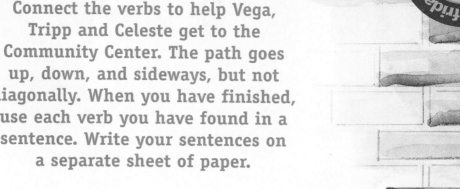

START

know	tell	come	well	each	into	she	there
my	one	wait	nod	friend	us	than	car
never	you	several	follow	lead	return	am	that
and	from	way	other	anything	to	say	about
see	smile	give	only	share	make	add	no
live	good	help	learn	have	shirt	every	cup
wave	they	wood	so	here	greet	stop	talk
visit	put	breathe	show	enter	explain	with	run

FINISH

Community Center

Totally Weird Plurals!

For most nouns, you need to add an "s" to make it plural.
However, there are always exceptions to the rules. Do you know
the plural forms of these words?

goose	geese
ox	_____
tooth	_____
deer	_____
person	_____
mouse	_____
man	_____
child	_____
foot	_____
sheep	_____
moose	_____

How many did you get right? _____
Now try this one!

duck-billed platypus _____

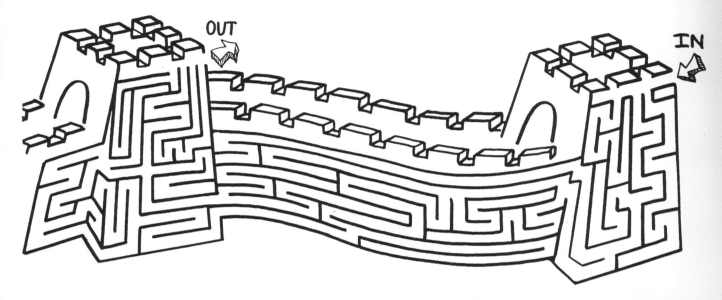

Possessive Pronouns

Possessive pronouns show ownership.
Example: **his** book, **her** bike, **our** house
You can use possessive pronouns in front of a noun or on their own.
Example: That is **my** paper.   That is **mine**.

Rewrite the sentences using possessive pronouns.

1. **The dog's dish is too full.** _____

2. **That toy is Sally's toy.** _____

3. **That cat is our cat.** _____

4. **Those shoes are Tony's shoes.** _____

Fishing for Homonyms

Homonyms are words that sound the same but have different meanings. Match these fishermen with the fish that sounds the same as the word on their boats.

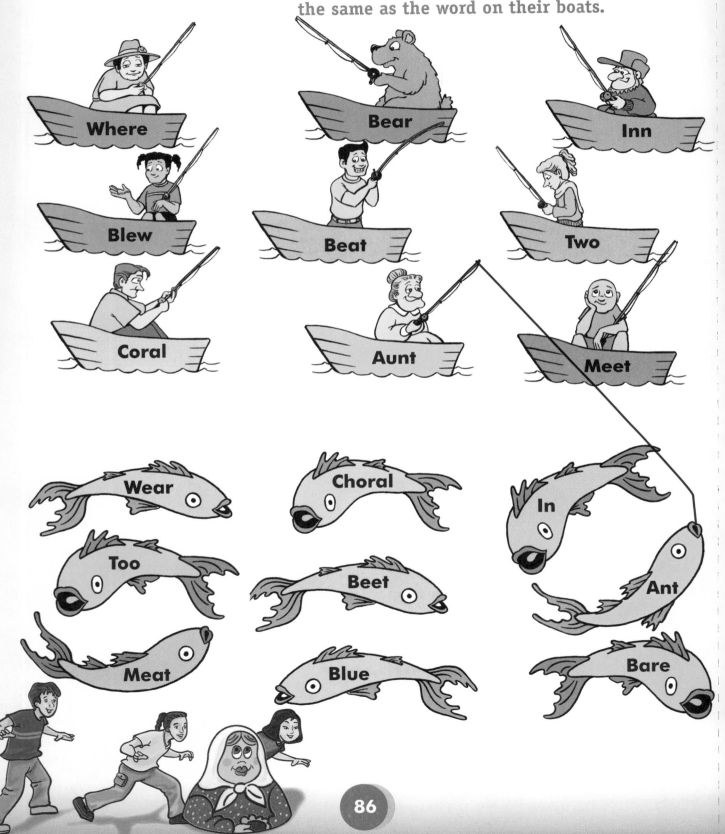

Where

Bear

Inn

Blew

Beat

Two

Coral

Aunt

Meet

Wear

Choral

In

Too

Beet

Ant

Meat

Blue

Bare

86

Journal

Use a blank sheet of paper if you need more space.

I'm thankful today because...

_____

_____

_____

_____

_____

_____

_____

_____

_____

_____

_____

_____

_____

_____

_____

_____

_____

_____

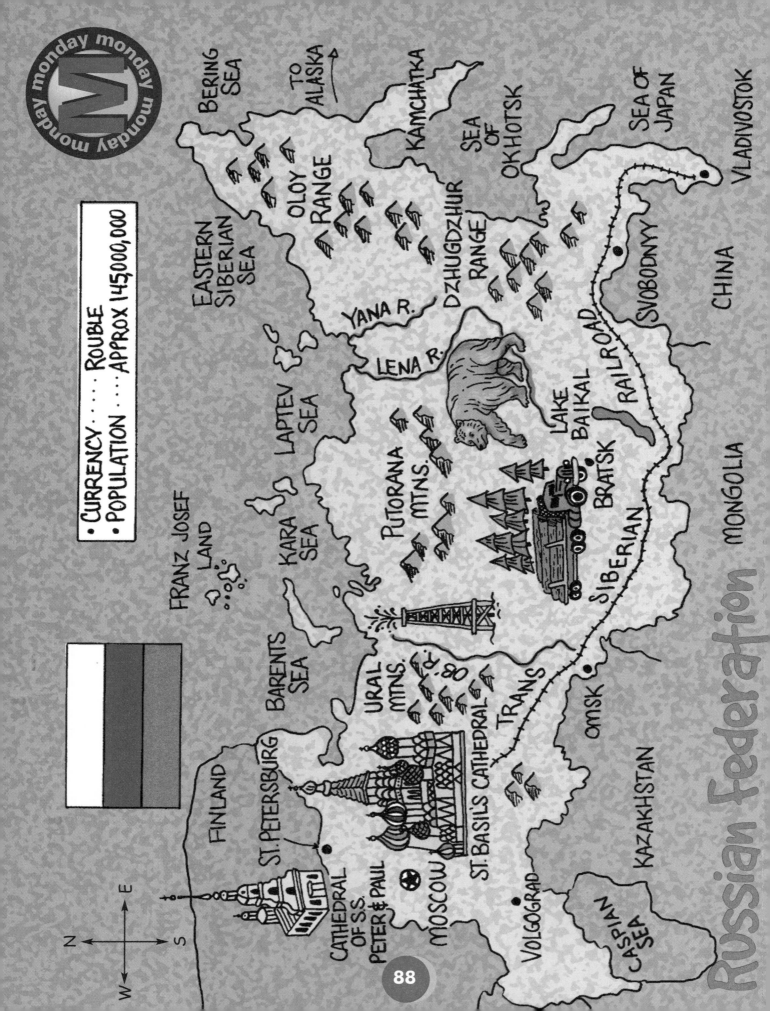

Russian Federation

Crossword

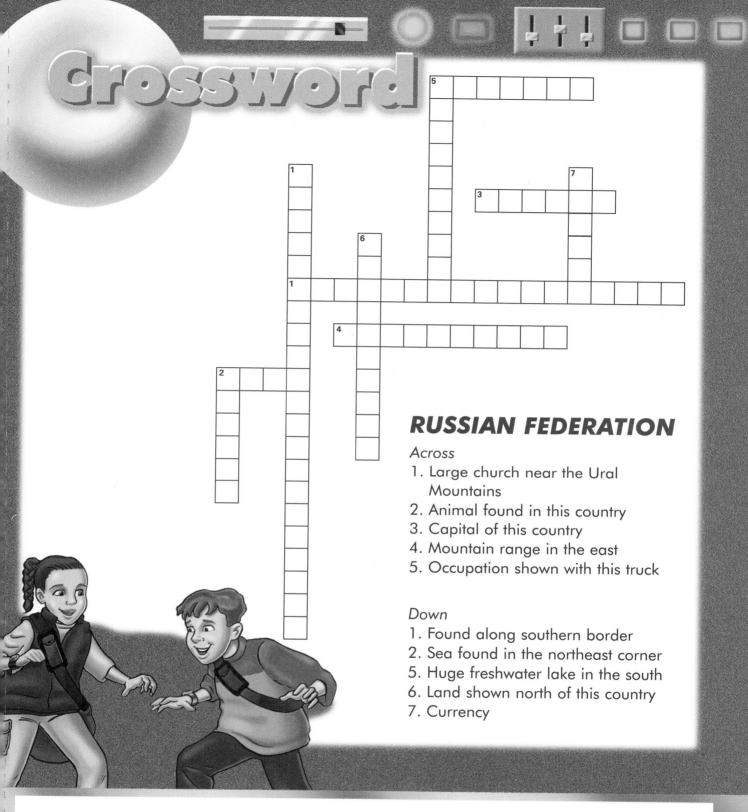

RUSSIAN FEDERATION

Across
1. Large church near the Ural Mountains
2. Animal found in this country
3. Capital of this country
4. Mountain range in the east
5. Occupation shown with this truck

Down
1. Found along southern border
2. Sea found in the northeast corner
5. Huge freshwater lake in the south
6. Land shown north of this country
7. Currency

Facts about Russian Federation

Russia stretches over Eastern Europe and Northern Asia. It is the world's largest country. Russia's currency is the rouble. Bears are native to this land. Russia produces one-fifth of the world's softwood, which makes logging an important industry. Want to learn more about Russia? **Visit http://www.interknowledge.com/russia/**

Addition and Subtraction with Decimals

Complete the equations below. The first one has been done for you.

1

$$
\begin{array}{r}
^1.982 \\
.741 \\
+\ \underline{.015} \\
1.738
\end{array}
$$

2

$$
\begin{array}{r}
.734 \\
-\ \underline{.322}
\end{array}
$$

3

$$
\begin{array}{r}
.229 \\
-\ \underline{.228}
\end{array}
$$

4

$$
\begin{array}{r}
.627 \\
.459 \\
+\ \underline{.333}
\end{array}
$$

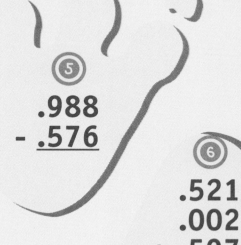

5

$$
\begin{array}{r}
.988 \\
-\ \underline{.576}
\end{array}
$$

6

$$
\begin{array}{r}
.521 \\
.002 \\
+\ \underline{.597}
\end{array}
$$

7

$$
\begin{array}{r}
.225 \\
.310 \\
+\ \underline{.427}
\end{array}
$$

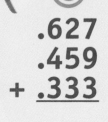

8

$$
\begin{array}{r}
.839 \\
-\ \underline{.608}
\end{array}
$$

Line 'Em Up!

Celeste, Vega and Tripp have collected pairs of dolls to display at the Community Center. Each pair weighs less than 4 pounds. Calculate their weight, then show where each number would be on the number line below. The first one has been done for you.

1.   1.54
   + 2.36
     3.90

2.   0.63
   + 0.77

3.   0.48
   + 0.29

4.   1.01
   + 0.08

5.   0.23
   + 0.65

6.   2.47
   + 0.89

7.   1.70
   + 0.96

8.   1.69
   + 1.29

9.   0.67
   + 0.98

10.   0.71
   + 2.44

3.90

0   1   2   3   4

91

Journal

Use a blank sheet of paper if you need more space.

Where is your favorite place to visit during the summer? Write an article for a travel magazine for kids describing this place. Make sure to include information about where it is, what they can do there, and what makes this place so great.

People Everywhere!

Celeste, Vega and Tripp have been studying the population of a number of countries. Using the graph below, answer the questions.

When you are finished, unscramble the letters below the answers you have selected to answer the question.

India - Over 1,000,000,000   Australia - Over 20,000,000

England - Over 59,000,000   China - Over 1,290,000,000

Egypt - Over 72,000,000   Russia - Over 145,000,000

Italy - Over 57,000,000

Which countries have over 1,000,000,000 people?	Russia R	China S	England T	India S
Which countries have less than 60,000,000 people?	Egypt N	Australia C	Russia E	Italy N
What country has the most people?	Russia A	China U	England P	India O
What country has the least number of people?	England O	Egypt A	Australia E	Russia S

Who Am I?

I am an official count of the population. The first one in the United States was taken in 1790, and there has been one every ten years since then.

What am I?

_____

Number Lines

Write the number that belongs where the question mark is on each of the number lines below.

1. 61 64 68 ? 72   ? =

2. 194 197 201 ? 207   ? =

3. -4 ? 0 2 4 6 8   ? =

4. -10 -8 -1 ? 1 2   ? =

5. 0.4 0.9 ? 1.3 1.7   ? =

6. 1.28 1.33 1.35 ? 1.40   ? =

weird science

There is enough water in the earth's atmosphere that if it all fell down at one time it would cover the whole globe with more than an inch (3 cm) of rain!

Math Games

Do you see a pattern? Fill in the blanks with the correct number to complete the pattern.

1. 6 12 ___ 48 96

2. 5 10 20 ___ 80

3. 7 14 ___ 56 112

4. 3 6 ___ 24 48

5. 9 ___ 36 72 144

6. 4 8 16 ___ 64

Wanted: Volunteers

Chapter 7

The group met early the next day to walk to the Center and update Ms. Darcy on their progress.

"Look at that!" Tripp pointed to a young man in an empty lot.

As the children watched, the wind eased and a triangular kite floated gracefully downward. The young man began winding up the string. He noticed the children watching and nodded his head in greeting.

"It's beautiful," called Celeste. "I've never seen a kite like that."

"Thanks. It's called a delta," said the man, walking toward them. "I'm Ken Kuo."

"Hi, I'm Celeste. I've seen you at my sister's school. My friends are Tripp and Vega. We really like your kite."

Ken smiled. "I just made it and came here to do a test flight."

"You made it?" exclaimed Vega.

Ken chuckled. "People have been making kites for a couple thousand years now. With just a few simple supplies, they're not too hard to make."

Celeste had an idea. "Ken, could you teach other people to make kites? Maybe even a bunch of people—at the Community Center?"

"Does the Center offer that kind of class?" asked Ken.

"It can if you'll teach it!" said Tripp. "You should talk to the director."

"I guess that would be all right," agreed Ken. "It might be fun."

As the three turned away, a city bus went past. One side of the bus displayed an ad for the zoo. Celeste froze. "Did you see those koalas? Come on, guys!"

Forgetting the Center, they ran to Celeste's house. Pushing open the front door, she called to her older sister. "Cassie? Can you go with us to the zoo tomorrow?"

Choose the correct definition of each word from the story. Circle the letter in front of your choice.

1. **empty**
   a. damp
   b. slow-moving
   c. containing nothing
   d. dirty

2. **triangular**
   a. having three sides
   b. with straight sides
   c. extra
   d. regular

3. **gracefully**
   a. straight
   b. with beautiful movement
   c. in a random way
   d. in a quick way

4. **chuckled**
   a. scowled
   b. cleared the throat
   c. snorted
   d. laughed softly

5. **couple**
   a. many
   b. none
   c. two
   d. a dozen

6. **simple**
   a. special
   b. easily done or used
   c. homemade
   d. costly

7. **supplies**
   a. equipment
   b. instructions
   c. money
   d. wooden sticks

8. **director**
   a. an elected official
   b. a volunteer
   c. a person who leads or guides
   d. creator

Fix the Facts

My friend Molly has been sending me letters in the mail.
She moved away a few months ago. I really miss her, but we keep
in touch by writing letters to each other. I save all Molly's letters so
I can read them again when I'm feeling lonely. Can you figure
out the order in which Molly sent the letters below to me?

A.

Hi Sue,

Did you get my letter about coming to school with me? Let me know if the date is okay with you.

Your friend,
Molly

B.

Hi Sue,

How are you doing? I am so glad you can come next Friday and spend the weekend. It will be great taking you to my new school.

Your friend,
Molly

C.

Hi Sue,

It's been three weeks since I moved! Thank you for calling me the other night. I really enjoyed our conversation. It was great to hear your voice. I can't wait until we can hang out again.

Your friend,
Molly

D.

Hi Sue,

I really miss you! I have been here a week now. I met some new friends. They seem very nice. Call me soon, okay? I hope you're fine.

Your friend,
Molly

E.

Hi Sue,

I can't believe it's been a month since I've moved away. Two weeks from Friday is "bring a guest to school day." I wonder if you want to be my guest? Let me know if you can come. I have to do my homework now.

Your friend,
Molly

F.

Hi Sue,

Thank you for coming to my school. It was great to get to hang out just like old times. Hope to see you soon.

Your friend,
Molly

1. _____   4. _____

2. _____   5. _____

3. _____   6. _____

IN

OUT

Correct the Sentences

Add the correct punctuation and capitalize the proper nouns and the beginning words of each sentence.

1. where are you going on vacation sally

2. we are going to my grandmas cottage in minnesota

3. i've heard it gets really really cold in minnesota

4. it is cold in the winter but the summers are warm

Making Deductions

Making a deduction is examining facts, thinking logically and coming to a conclusion.

Read the sentence below and make a deduction.

1. Angela went to the store at lunch. Bert went to the store after dinner. Karen went to the store 2 hours before Bert. Who went to the store first?

2. Scott has a pet he keeps in a tank. Susan's pet flies in its cage. Victor's pet walks on a leash. Who has a pet turtle?

3. Evan got a silver medal in the race. Bob ran faster than Evan. Jim's time was slower than Evan's. Who won the gold medal in the race?

4. Kim used a spoon to eat her lunch. Tammy's lunch was inside of a bag. Terry needed a fork for his lunch. Who had the sandwich?

5. Megan's favorite fruit grows on a vine. Leslie's favorite fruit grows on a tree. Sara's favorite fruit has seeds on the outside? Whose favorite fruit is apples?

6. Tim, John and Mike all like to play sports. Tim's favorite sport involves a hoop. John's favorite sport uses a racquet. Mike's favorite sport involves kicking a ball. Whose favorite sport is tennis?

Journal

Use a blank sheet of paper if you need more space.

I'm thankful today because...

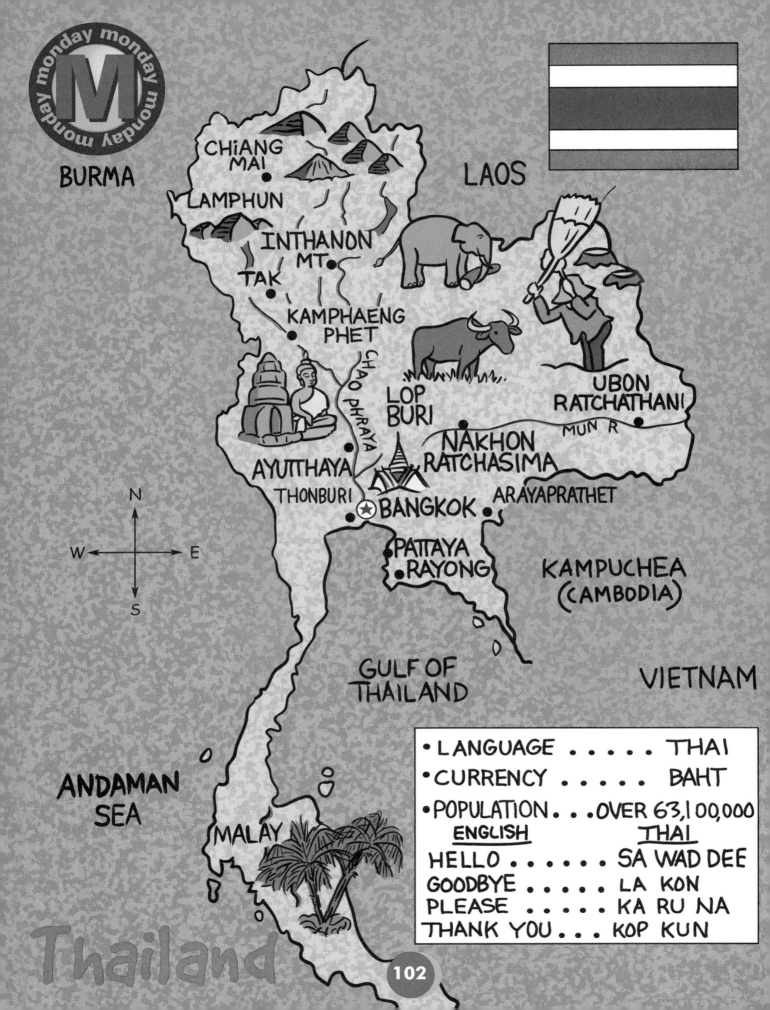

BURMA

CHIANG MAI

LAMPHUN

INTHANON MT.

TAK

KAMPHAENG PHET

CHAO PHRAYA

AYUTTHAYA

THONBURI

LAOS

UBON RATCHATHANI

MUN R

LOP BURI

NAKHON RATCHASIMA

ARAYAPRATHET

BANGKOK

PATTAYA
RAYONG

KAMPUCHEA (CAMBODIA)

VIETNAM

N
W   E
S

GULF OF THAILAND

ANDAMAN SEA

MALAY

Thailand

• LANGUAGE . . . . . . THAI
• CURRENCY . . . . . BAHT
• POPULATION . . . OVER 63,100,000

ENGLISH	THAI
HELLO	SA WAD DEE
GOODBYE	LA KON
PLEASE	KA RU NA
THANK YOU . . .	KOP KUN

Crossword

THAILAND

Across

1. During Thailand's monsoon season, lots of _____ falls every day.
2. The central plains of Thailand are covered with _____ paddies. This small white grain is a staple of the Thai diet.
3. In northern Thailand, these enormous animals are used to haul lumber out of the mountain forests.
4. _____ is a beautiful and expensive fabric that is a main export of Thailand. It is made of fine fibers that are spun by worms.

Down

1. Many Thai people live in houses built on stilts along the Chao Phraya, which is a main _____ in Thailand.
2. Thailand is located in the southeast portion of this continent.
3. _____ is the capital and largest city in Thailand.
4. On farms in southern Thailand, monkeys are trained to climb tall palm trees to help harvest these large, brown, hard-shelled fruits.

Facts about Thailand

Thailand is located in Southeast Asia. Bangkok is the capital and largest city in Thailand. Thailand gets lots of rain during the monsoon season. The Chao Phraya is a main river in Thailand where many people live in houses built on stilts. The central plains are covered with rice paddies. Rice is a staple of the Thai diet. Silk, spun by worms, is a main export. Thai people use animals to help with their work. Elephants haul lumber out of the mountain forests in the north and monkeys help harvest coconuts in the south. Find out about Thailand from kids just like you! **Visit http://www.thaistudents.com** Take tours of the palaces in Thailand. **Visit http://www.palaces.thai.net/**

Measuring Area and Perimeter

Area measures the number of square units needed to cover something.
Perimeter measures the distance around something.

Measure the area in square units and the perimeter in units (one side of the square unit) for the shapes below:

Example

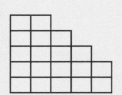

Area   = <u> 8 </u>

Perimeter = <u> 14 </u>

 ①

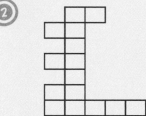 ②

Area   = _____

Perimeter = _____

Area   = _____

Perimeter = _____

 ③

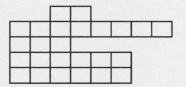

 ④

Area   = _____

Perimeter = _____

Area   = _____

Perimeter = _____

 ⑤

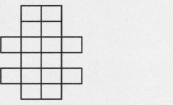

 ⑥

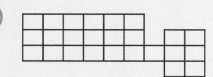

Area   = _____

Perimeter = _____

Area   = _____

Perimeter = _____

Looney Zoo!

Look at the map of the zoo that Celeste and Vega got when they went with Cassie. What is the area and perimeter of each exhibit?

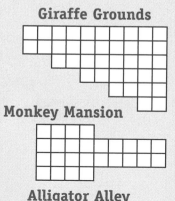

Giraffe Grounds

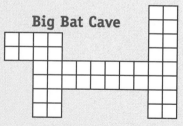

Big Bat Cave

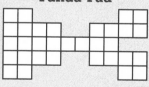

Panda Pad

Monkey Mansion

Kangaroo Outback

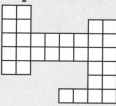

Elephant Heaven

Alligator Alley

Zebra Zone

● You are here

Giraffe Grounds

Area = _____

Perimeter = _____

Monkey Mansion

Area = _____

Perimeter = _____

Alligator Alley

Area = _____

Perimeter = _____

Panda Pad

Area = _____

Perimeter = _____

Big Bat Cave

Area = _____

Perimeter = _____

Kangaroo Outback

Area = _____

Perimeter = _____

Zebra Zone

Area = _____

Perimeter = _____

Elephant Heaven

Area = _____

Perimeter = _____

Journal

Use a blank sheet of paper if you need more space.

Are there things that many people don't know about you that you wish they did? What would be a good question to ask you? Come up with three questions you want people to ask you and then answer them truthfully.

State of Affairs!

Celeste, Vega and Tripp have been studying how different atoms and molecules are arranged in all *matter*. Matter is anything that takes up space. The way these tiny little molecules are arranged determines an object's *state of matter*. The three states of matter we see around us on Earth are *solid*, *liquid* and *gas*. A *solid* is something that has a definite size and shape. A *liquid* takes on the shape of its container. (For example, the liquid inside of a cup takes on the shape of the cup.) A *gas* is matter that doesn't have a definite shape or definite size.

Help them decide the *state of matter* for each object. When you are finished, unscramble the letters below the answers you have selected to answer the question.

Steam from a cup of tea	Solid A	Liquid C	Gas E
A Brass key	Solid H	Liquid O	Gas D
Orange Juice	Solid T	Liquid M	Gas S
Oil	Solid R	Liquid I	Gas A
Oxygen inside of a tank	Solid B	Liquid A	Gas U
Doorknob	Solid L	Liquid C	Gas N

Guess Who I Am!

I am colorless, odorless and tasteless. I often fill up balloons to give them a little lift. What am I?

Rounding

Round the following numbers to the nearest hundred. If the number has five tens or more, round it up to the next highest hundred. If it has four tens or less, round it down to the nearest hundred.

Examples: 125 → 100   192 → 200

1. 559 → _____

2. 471 → _____

3. 812 → _____

4. 939 → _____

5. 678 → _____

6. 381 → _____

7. 261 → _____

8. 751 → _____

9. 174 → _____

10. 632 → _____

11. 851 → _____

12. 742 → _____

13. 715 → _____

14. 688 → _____

weird science

Everyone's heard of black holes in space. Did you know black holes are so dense that nothing can escape their gravity? Not even light!

Math Games

Each shape has a value. Scales 1 and 2 are in perfect balance.
How many circles are needed to balance scales 3, 4, 5, 6, 7 and 8?

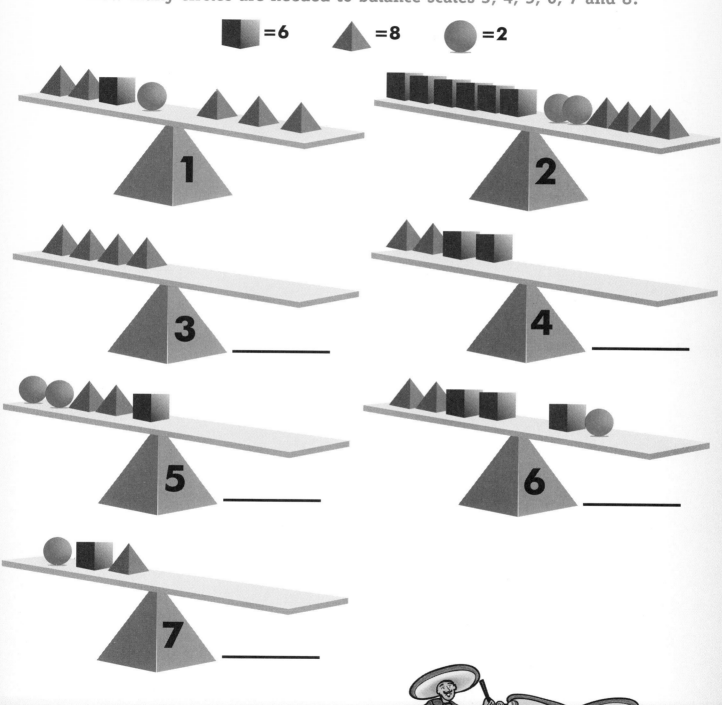

=6   =8   =2

Wanted: Volunteers

Chapter 8

Cassie, Vega and Celeste were the first in line for the zoo. Tripp, still being mysterious, was busy with another errand and unable to join them.

"The kangaroos are over there!" Celeste was so eager to see the Australian exhibit that she almost dragged her sister Cassie along.

"Here they are! Look how pretty their eyes are!" Celeste leaned over a fence, wanting to get closer.

"I'd say pretty fast," said Vega, reading a large plaque. "Kangaroos can go 40 miles an hour. What would that be in kilometers, Celeste?"

"That would be...about 64.37 kilometers per hour."

"Thank you, Miss Calculator," teased Vega.

After watching the kangaroos quietly nibble on grass, the girls headed for the office. Once there, Cassie, Vega and Celeste were taken to the zoo's community coordinator, Mrs. Craig. Celeste explained how they were recruiting volunteers for the Community Center and how much she liked kangaroos.

Mrs. Craig asked, "Would you like to add the Touring Zoo to your list?"

"The Touring Zoo?" Celeste looked blank.

"It's a bus that travels around to teach about the zoo's programs and animals. It sounds as if you'd like some wallabies aboard."

"Wallabies?" wondered Vega and Celeste.

Mrs. Craig smiled. "They're a smaller version of a kangaroo. They fit on the bus better." Everyone laughed. "Have your Community Center director fill out these papers."

"Thank you," said Celeste. Vega froze as the children walked out. She pointed at the advertisement on the bus stop bench. "Come to the Rain Forest. See Brazil."

Cassie knew what Celeste and Vega were thinking. "I can't go tomorrow, but we can go the day after." They made plans to visit the Natural History Museum.

Chapter 8

Skill: Adverbs

To answer each question,
find the adverb in the story.
Adverbs tell how, when or where
something happened. The first
one has been done for you.

1. How did the kangaroos nibble on grass? _____QUIETLY_____

2. Where are the kangaroos? _____

3. How eager was Celeste? _____

4. Where does the zoo bus travel? _____

5. Where do the children walk? _____

6. When can't Cassie go to the museum? _____

Now complete these sentences. Use adverbs to tell how, when
or where the action happened.

7. The other day I walked _____ (tell how) down the sidewalk.

8. Mom moved my fish tank _____ (tell where).

9. I read the greatest book _____ (tell when).

10. "Lisa," said Larue _____ (tell how), "come here."

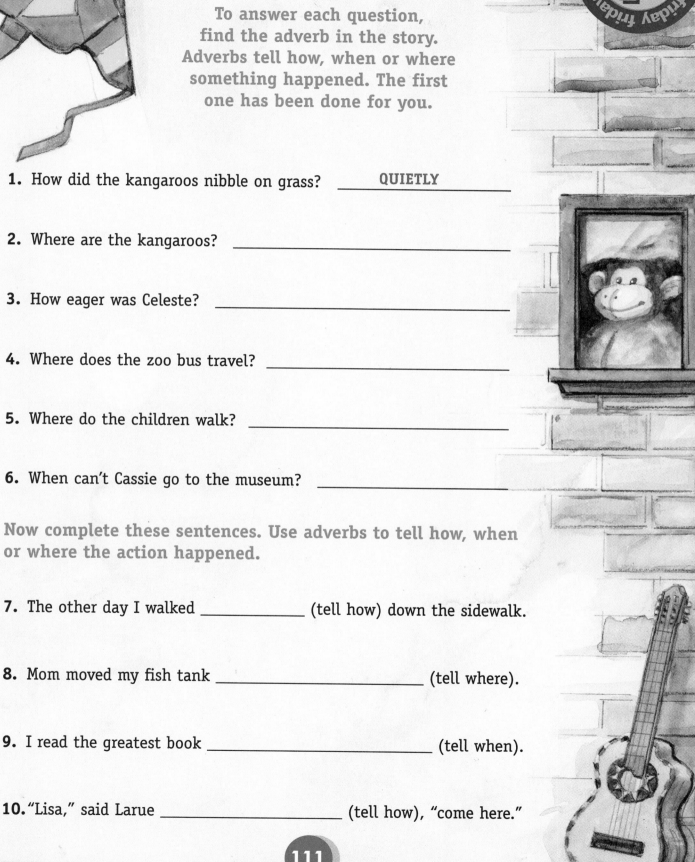

CRAZY CAPERS

Who Robbed Oakville Bank?

Someone robbed Oakville Bank and it is up to Officer Chen to catch the criminal. He interviewed three witnesses. Because their memories were a little foggy, the witnesses each remembered one thing correctly and another one incorrectly. Based on the statements from the witnesses below, can you help Officer Chen determine who the bank robber is?

Witness #1: He had a beard and sunglasses.

Witness #2: He wasn't wearing sunglasses or a hat.

Witness #3: He didn't have a beard, but he did wear a hat.

Detective School Tip!

Each witness is saying two things about the suspect but one of them is not true. That means that both statements can't be true. So any suspect who fits both statements of one of the witnesses can't be the criminal! You can cross those suspects off your list! Witness #1 says the suspect had a beard and sunglasses. So any suspect who has BOTH a beard and sunglasses can be crossed off the list!

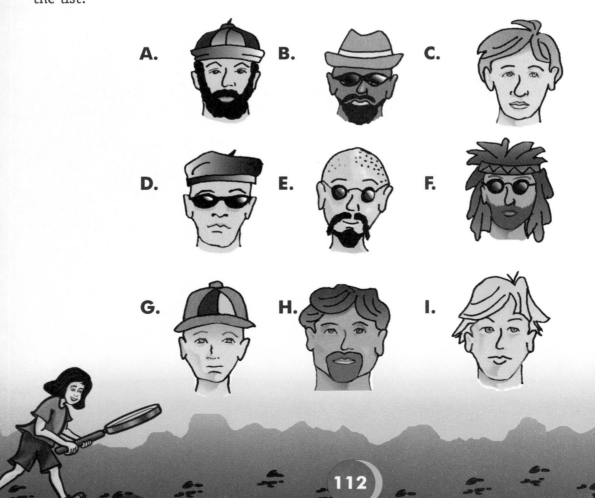

IN

OUT

Subject - Verb Agreement

Circle the correct verb for each sentence.

1. Sara (runs, ran) to the store yesterday.

2. Randy (will go, went) to school tomorrow.

3. Rachel (photographs, will photograph) the animals at the zoo next month.

4. The student (finished, finish) the test first.

Combine the Sentences

Combine each set of sentences into one. The first one is done for you.

1. Mary planted flowers yesterday. Mary is my friend.

_____Mary, my friend, planted flowers yesterday._____.

2. Joe is really tall. Joe is my brother.

_____.

3. Fred is a policeman. Fred is my uncle.

_____.

4. Bob is my neighbor. Bob mows his lawn on Sunday.

_____.

5. Frances likes to dance. Frances is my cousin.

_____.

6. Jan likes dogs. Jan is Jim's brother.

_____.

7. Steve likes to watch movies. Steve is my friend.

_____.

8. Dolphins live in the ocean. Dolphins are my favorite animal.

_____.

9. David plays baseball. David is my coach's son.

_____.

114

Journal

Use a blank sheet of paper if you need more space.

I'm thankful today because...

_____

_____

_____

_____

_____

_____

_____

_____

_____

_____

_____

_____

_____

_____

_____

_____

_____

_____

Crossword

BRAZIL

Across
1. Yellow fruit grown here
2. Very popular sport
3. River running east-west
5. This city is on the Atlantic Ocean
7. "Hello" in native language

Down
1. Town near Venezuela
4. Big-beaked birds
6. Currency

Facts about Brazil

Brazil is located in South America and is the fifth largest country in the world. Brasilia is the capital but Rio de Janeiro, located on the Atlantic Ocean, used to be the capital. Bananas and coffee are grown in Brazil and toucans, big-beaked birds, are native to Brazil. Ever wonder how people live in Brazil? **Visit http://www.brazil.org.uk/category.php?catid=67**

Place Value

Write the correct number on each line. The first one is done for you.

	100,000s	10,000s	1,000s	100s	10s	1s
1.	///// //	///	///// /	//	///	///// ///
2.	/	///// ////	////	/////	///// //	/
3.	///// //	///// /	///// ///	//	///	////
4.	//	////	///// //	/	//	///// ///
5.	///// ////	///	///// ////	/////	////	///// //
6.	////	///// ////	/	/////	//	/
7.	///	/////	///// /	/	///// //	///
8.	///// ///	/	////	///// /	//	///// ////

1. __736,238__   5. _____

2. _____   6. _____

3. _____   7. _____

4. _____   8. _____

Number Crunch!

Celeste told Vega that a kangaroo can run 64.37 kilometers per hour. 64.37 is written in *standard notation*. Did you know that you can break these numbers apart and write them in *expanded notation*? 60 + 4 + .3 + .07

Now give it a try. Write the following numbers in expanded notation. The first one has been done for you.

1. 89.58   **Expanded Notation:** 80 + 9 + .5 + .08

2. 875   **Expanded Notation:** _____

3. 765.4   **Expanded Notation:** _____

4. 1,265   **Expanded Notation:** _____

5. 997.2   **Expanded Notation:** _____

6. 45.07   **Expanded Notation:** _____

7. 803.2   **Expanded Notation:** _____

8. 770.05   **Expanded Notation:** _____

9. 400.25   **Expanded Notation:** _____

Journal

Use a blank sheet of paper if you need more space.

Do you ever wonder what it would be like to be a grown-up? If you could be grown-up right now, what would you want to be? What would you do?

Measure Making!

Celeste, Vega and Tripp have decided to bake some cookies to thank Mrs. Craig for her help at the zoo. While cooking, the three realized they needed many tools to measure *length*, *weight* and *volume*. *Length* measures how long something is. *Weight* measures the mass of an object. *Volume* measures how much space it takes up.

Help them decide what tool would be necessary to measure each item. When you are finished, unscramble the letters below the answers you have selected to answer the question.

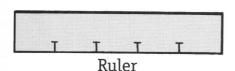
Ruler

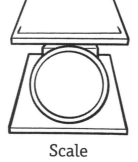
Scale

Measuring Cup

The length of the cookie sheet	Ruler C	Scale R	Measuring cup O
The amount of sugar	Ruler S	Scale E	Measuring cup B
The weight of the butter	Ruler T	Scale A	Measuring cup P
The amount of flour	Ruler M	Scale O	Measuring cup S
The weight of the chocolate chips	Ruler F	Scale A	Measuring cup W
The diameter of the cookies	Ruler U	Scale E	Measuring cup R

Guess Who I Am!
The Chinese have used me for thousands of years as a computing device. I am made of a frame holding parallel rods with counters that have beads you can move. I am an ancient calculator. What am I?

Number Words

Directions: Write each of these numbers in word form.
The first one has been done for you.

1. 72,348   <u>seventy-two thousand, three-hundred and forty-eight</u>

2. 36,692   _____

3. 102,355   _____

4. 98,006   _____

5. 4,908   _____

6. 45,321   _____

7. 220,063   _____

8. 28,414   _____

weird science

The sun is so hot it is estimated that the core is at least 25,000,000 degrees Fahrenheit (14,000,000 degrees Celsius)! That's hot!

Math Games

Do you see a pattern? Fill in the blanks with the correct number to complete the pattern.

1.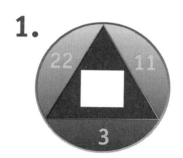

2.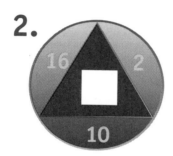

3.

4.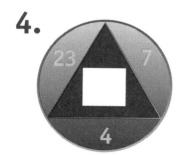

5.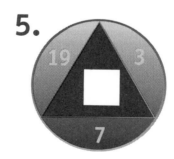

6.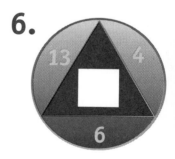

123

Wanted: Volunteers

Chapter 9

All were present for their trip to the museum. Slowly, they looked at each exhibit.

"Wow," said Vega. The walls seemed to have huge tree trunks growing from them. And the ceiling was a never-ending mass of branches and leaves.

Hidden television screens showed pictures of colorful and unusual animals and birds. And the sounds! The children had never heard such hoots and screeches.

Tripp read from a poster. "It says that Brazil has the third-largest block of rain forest in the world. But 13,000 square kilometers are cut or burned down every year. What is that in square miles, Celeste?"

She closed her eyes. "About 5,019.33 square miles."

"Can I help you?" Celeste jumped. A museum guide had come up behind her.

Celeste laid out their plans for the Community Center. The guide listened patiently and then said, "Come with me, please."

They followed him to the assistant director's office. Inside, he spoke to Mr. Tanner for a moment and then introduced everyone.

"Clark explained your plans," he said. "We don't usually do this, but all the rain forest branches, animals, and displays you saw have to go into storage next week. Maybe you could store some of them at your Community Center for a while?"

Vega was the first to respond. "Thank you!" Tripp gave Mr. Tanner the Center's phone number so he could talk to Ms. Darcy.

Later, Tripp, Vega and Celeste celebrated in Vega's living room. Vega noticed messages on the answering machine. The first was from Ms. Darcy asking them to come to her office the next morning.

A second message was from Tripp's mom, asking him to come home. Something big was waiting for him.

Skill: Adjectives

**Answer these questions
about Chapter 9. Use adjectives
for your answers.**

1. What kind of tree trunks seemed to grow out of the walls?

    _____

2. What kind of animals showed on the screens?

    _____

3. How many square miles did Celeste calculate?

    _____

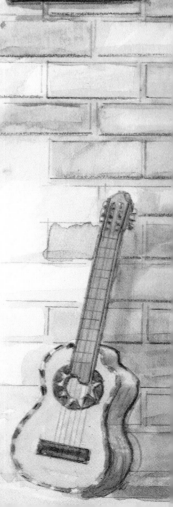

4. In which week does the display have to go into storage?

    _____

5. In which room were the children celebrating?

    _____

6. On which morning are the children to meet Ms. Darcy?

    _____

Challenge

In this chapter, Celeste used mental math to make difficult calculations. Use the following formula to change miles to kilometers: m X 1.609 = km

1. 80 miles = _____ km

2. 120 miles = _____ km

3. 10 miles = _____ km

Fix the Facts

Tara's mom told her that she could plan her birthday party all by herself. As a helpful hint, her mom told Tara to keep notes of her ideas so she wouldn't forget them. Tara did keep notes, but she didn't bother keeping them in order. Can you help Tara put her notes in order so she can review them?

A.
My birthday is in two weeks and my mom said I could plan it all by myself. I'm taking notes so I don't forget anything. The first thing I need to do is decide on a theme and make a list of people to invite.

B.
Today I filled out my invitations. My party will be next Saturday afternoon at 2:00 p.m. I am inviting nine friends. The next thing I need to do is order the cake this morning. I think I'll make it my favorite, chocolate!

C.
My mom and I are going to pick up the cake this morning. Everything else is set. My dad helped me put up the decorations and my little brother helped with the party favors. Planning a party is a lot of work!

D.
Today I asked my mom if she knew of a good bakery where I could order a cake. She told me she'd take care of the ordering if I told her what type of cake I wanted. I said I wanted it to be chocolate with cats on it. I hope it tastes good and looks good, too!

E.
I found the cutest invitations. They have all kinds of cats and kittens on them. I will begin filling them out soon. First I need to decide what time to have my party.

F.
I decided I want cats as my theme. I want decorations with cats, a cake with cats, and invitations with cats. I love cats! I'm going to the store with my mom tonight to see if we can find decorations and invitations with cats on them.

1. _____   4. _____

2. _____   5. _____

3. _____   6. _____

OUT

IN

MAZE

Unscramble the Geography

Listed below are names of the countries from the geography sections on Monday. Unscramble the names. Remember to capitalize the first letter.

1. gtpye _____

2. zrbail _____

3. udntie gidknmo _____

4. saaruilta _____

5. nciha _____

6. nadii _____

7. yltia _____

8. dniaahtl _____

Fact vs. Opinion
Facts can be proven to be true.
Opinions express what someone thinks or feels.

Decide if each statement below is a fact or an opinion.

1. The spelling quiz had 100 words.   *fact/opinion*

2. Bob is the best baseball player in the world.   *fact/opinion*

3. Downhill skiing is easy to learn.   *fact/opinion*

4. Mary visited Toronto with her family on vacation.   *fact/opinion*

5. Her mom bakes the best apple pies.   *fact/opinion*

6. That car has a flat tire.   *fact/opinion*

7. She woke up at 7:00 a.m.   *fact/opinion*

8. Iguanas make the best pets.   *fact/opinion*

9. It's fun to go swimming in the ocean.   *fact/opinion*

10. The store is closed this weekend.   *fact/opinion*

Journal

Use a blank sheet of paper if you need more space.

I'm thankful today because...

Crossword

GREECE

Across
1. Mountains located in the west
2. Island west of Samos
3. Sea on the east coast
4. Island south of Lesvos

Down
1. Popular landmark in Athens
2. Sea to the west
4. Island to the south
5. Island off the coast of Albania
6. River south of Mt. Olympus

Facts about Greece

Greece is located in southern Europe. Numerous islands and the Aegean Sea surround it to the east, the Ionian Sea to the west and the Mediterranean Sea to the south. Athens is the capital and the home of the Parthenon. Learn about the ancient Greek cities of Olympia, Athens and Corinth. **Visit http://www.bbc.co.uk/schools/ancientgreece/**

Multiplication and Division

Complete the equations below.

①
```
  324
x   6
```

②
```
4 | 284
```

③
```
3 | 336
```

④
```
  119
x   3
```

⑤
```
  511
x   6
```

⑥
```
7 | 497
```

⑦
```
  226
x   5
```

⑧
```
9 | 819
```

132

...And Bingo is the Game! Oh!

Celeste, Vega and Tripp decided to play a game of Bingo. Only one of them won. Use the problems next to each person's name to see what numbers they got. If the answer appears on their card, cross out the number.

Celeste

1. 6 x 8   2. 63 ÷ 9   3. 4 x 7   4. 8 x 8   5. 24 ÷ 6   6. 3 x 9

Vega

7. 8 x 3   8. 5 x 7   9. 64 ÷ 8   10. 18 ÷ 2   11. 6 x 6   12. 7 x 3

Tripp

13. 24 ÷ 12   14. 8 x 4   15. 36 ÷ 9   16. 7 x 8   17. 7 x 2   18. 27 ÷ 9

Who won? _____

Celeste

B	I	N	G	O
48	6	7	15	3
21	16	42	18	27
9	1	Free Space	5	13
45	5	65	28	58
40	11	64	66	44

Vega

B	I	N	G	O
24	1	56	14	81
19	35	3	7	9
16	41	Free Space	43	19
54	11	8	36	26
29	34	46	52	21

Tripp

B	I	N	G	O
19	58	42	36	7
0	14	56	8	3
5	32	Free Space	13	36
40	35	4	18	22
21	64	27	32	15

Journal

Use a blank sheet of paper if you need more space.

Who is your best friend? What makes them special to you? Write a letter to your best friend explaining what you like about them and why you enjoy being with them.

Unlock the Rock!

Celeste, Vega and Tripp are meeting with Dr. Martin, a paleontologist, to see if she would be interested in volunteering at the Community Center. A paleontologist is a scientist that studies fossils. Fossils are the remains of past life, usually found in rocks. The remains can be fossils of plants or animals.

You can be a paleontologist! Help Celeste, Vega and Tripp determine what each of the fossils on the left used to be by circling the correct answer on the right. When you are finished, unscramble the letters below the answers you have selected to answer the question.

	B	T	E
	O	A	I
	A	R	S
	Y	T	S
	R	M	N
	O	A	E

Guess Who I Am!

I am an edible mollusk with 2 shells. I evolved in the Jurassic era. What am I?

_____

135

Story Problem

Solve the story problem below.

It is 4:00 p.m. Your friend called you to go to the movies at 5:30 p.m. You have to finish your homework first. You have 20 math problems left to do and they take you three minutes each to complete.

How long will it take you to finish?

_____

What time will you be done?

_____

If it takes 15 minutes to get to the movie theater, what time will you get to the movies?

_____

Will you be able to make it to the movies on time?

_____

weird science

Have you heard of the speed of light? Well, light is pretty fast; 300,000 kilometers (186,400 miles) per second as a matter of fact!

Math Games

Do you see a pattern? Fill in the blanks with the correct numbers to complete the pattern.

1. 50   45   40   ___   30

2. 66   60   ___   48   42

3. 82   ___   66   58   50

4. 55   ___   41   34   27

5. 43   37   ___   25   19

6. 68   60   52   44   ___

Wanted: Volunteers

Chapter 10

"Good morning, volunteers," said Ms. Darcy cheerfully. "Yesterday, my son introduced me to his class's new exchange student. I think you'll like him." She opened her office door.

A tall, slender teenager came in. "Peter, these are the volunteers I told you about—Vega, Tripp and Celeste." Peter said hello and shook hands with the children, which made them feel like grown-ups.

"How can I help?" asked Peter. Eyebrows went up. So this was what Ms. Darcy had up her sleeve. Peter was from England!

Tripp thought out loud. "It would be great if you talked about England. It's too bad we don't have any pictures." The girls agreed.

"Actually, I do have pictures—at least at home I do," Peter volunteered. "I backpacked around a bit last summer and took dozens of them. I could share my pictures of Stonehenge and Buckingham Palace."

"What are those?" asked Vega.

"Stonehenge is a mysterious prehistoric monument that was built over 5,000 years ago. Buckingham Palace is where the royal monarchs live. The queen uses the palace to do business and entertain guests," said Peter. "My pictures are all digital; I could have my mum e-mail them."

Celeste turned to Ms. Darcy. "Could he use a computer to display the photos?"

"I can see to that," said Ms. Darcy with a smile.

Vega, Tripp and Celeste responded in unison, "Add him to the list!"

Later, over lunch, Tripp added Mr. Tanner, Ken Kuo, and Peter to the list of recruits. Vega looked over Tripp's shoulder.

"There's just one more place to go," she said.

Skill: Reading Comprehension

Use the clues from the story to solve this crossword puzzle.

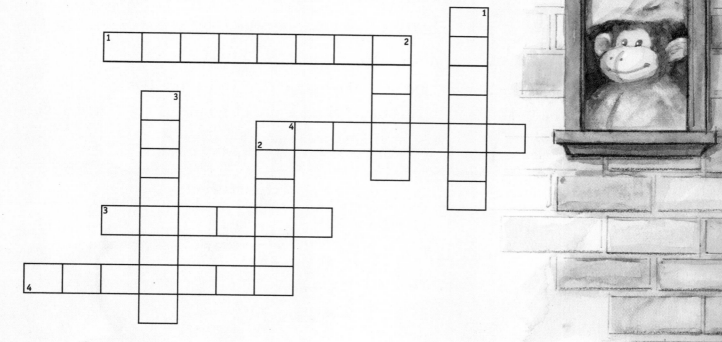

Across

1. Peter is an _____ student.

2. Peter's kind of pictures.

3. Season when Peter backpacked.

4. What Vega, Celeste and Tripp are.

Down

1. Where Peter is from.

2. How Peter's mum will send photos.

3. Machine for displaying photos.

4. Number of Peter's pictures.

A Picture's Worth a Thousand Words

Did you ever have to describe what someone looked like? If so, you used adjectives without even knowing it. Adjectives are words that describe. They can tell about shape, color, size, mood, and much more.

Look at the following sentences:

The **tall, dark-haired** man wore **brown** shoes.

The words "tall" and "dark-haired" are adjectives that describe the man.

The word "brown" is an adjective that describes the color of his shoes.

Find a photo from a magazine or a newspaper that you think looks really interesting and staple it to this page. Make a list of nouns you see in the picture and then make a list of adjectives that describe each noun in your list.

Nouns	Adjectives

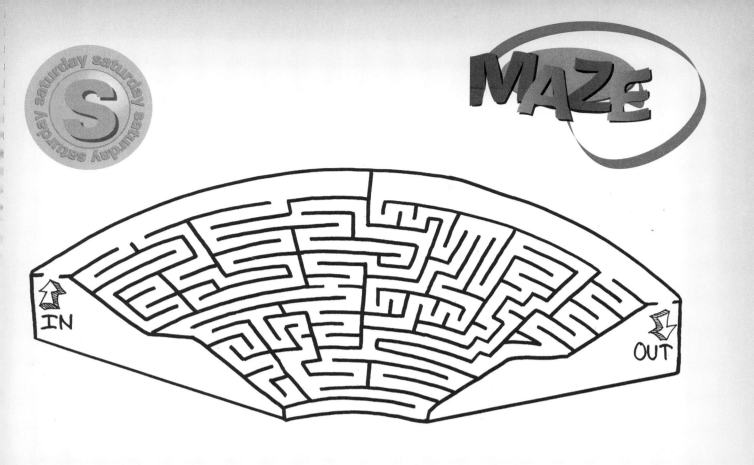

Complete Sentences

Read the sentences below and decide if they are complete (contain subject and verb) or if they are incomplete.

1. The old wise man.   complete/incomplete

2. The championship horse won the race. complete/incomplete

3. Running quickly on the playground.   complete/incomplete

4. The report cards were mailed home.   complete/incomplete

CRAZY CAPERS

Who broke the eggs?

Jordan had been keeping an eye on the bird's nest outside of his bedroom window hoping to see the babies hatch. Unfortunately, when he awoke this morning he noticed that the nest had been disturbed. Two of the eggs had crashed to the ground and broken. Based on the clues below, can you help Jordan figure out who, or what, climbed the tree and disturbed the nest?

Was it...

- A mouse
- Jamison, Jordan's bratty brother
- A snake
- A rat

- A cat
- An eagle
- Jamison's pet iguana
- A squirrel
- The phone repair person

CLUES!!!

1. It is not a reptile.

2. It has claws.

3. It is a mammal.

4. It is not a rodent.

Journal

Use a blank sheet of paper if you need more space.

I'm thankful today because...

_____

_____

_____

_____

_____

_____

_____

_____

_____

_____

_____

_____

_____

_____

_____

_____

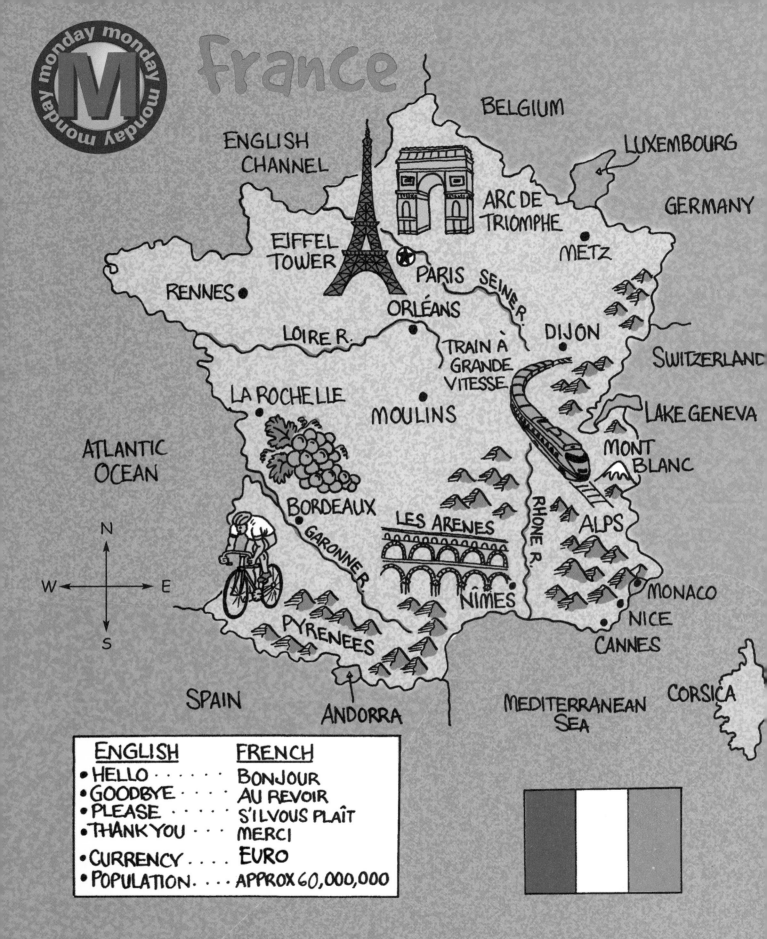

France

ENGLISH CHANNEL

BELGIUM

LUXEMBOURG

GERMANY

ARC DE TRIOMPHE

EIFFEL TOWER

METZ

RENNES

PARIS

SEINE R.

ORLÉANS

DIJON

SWITZERLAND

LOIRE R.

TRAIN À GRANDE VITESSE

LA ROCHELLE

MOULINS

LAKE GENEVA

MONT BLANC

ATLANTIC OCEAN

BORDEAUX

GARONNE R.

LES ARENES

RHONE R.

ALPS

N

W — E

S

PYRENEES

NÎMES

MONACO

NICE

CANNES

SPAIN

ANDORRA

MEDITERRANEAN SEA

CORSICA

ENGLISH	FRENCH
• HELLO	BONJOUR
• GOODBYE	AU REVOIR
• PLEASE	S'IL VOUS PLAÎT
• THANK YOU	MERCI
• CURRENCY	EURO
• POPULATION	APPROX 60,000,000

Crossword

FRANCE

Across

1. Very famous tower in Paris
3. Not a "mean" city
4. Orleans lies along this river
6. Fruit grown near Bordeaux
8. Approximately 60,000,000 is the what of this country?

Down

2. The capital lies along this river
5. Sport shown near the Pyrenees
7. Famous mountains along the southeastern border

Facts about France

France is located in Europe. Paris, the capital, lies along the Seine River. Paris has many famous landmarks including the Eiffel Tower and Arc de Triomphe. France is famous for its wine. Grapes to make wine are grown near Bordeaux. Ever visit the Eiffel Tower? Take a virtual tour at the official site **http://www.tour-eiffel.fr/teiffel/uk/** Learn all about France by visiting this website made just for kids! **http://www.info-france-usa.org/kids/**

What Is the Probability?

Probability is the measure of how likely something is going to happen. You can describe the events by using these words: *certain, more likely, equally likely, less likely,* or *impossible.*

If you were to pull out one ball from each of the bags, what is the probability of pulling out a green ball on the first try?

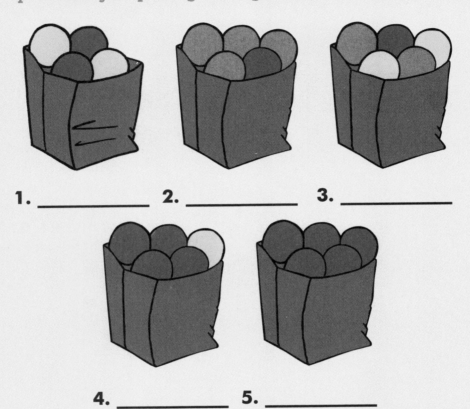

1. _____   2. _____   3. _____

4. _____   5. _____

Now, what is the probability of each of these events occurring? Use one of the following words:

Certain   Very likely   Likely   Not likely   Impossible

6. The sun will rise tomorrow morning. _____

7. There will be a snowstorm tomorrow. _____

8. It will rain tomorrow. _____

9. It will be sunny tomorrow. _____

10. There will be a full moon tonight. _____

Shape Up!

Can You Find The Same Pictures?

Vega and Tripp have decided to help Celeste finish her mural. Celeste needs their help to put on shapes that are *congruent*. Two objects are *congruent* if they are the same shape and size. They do not have to be facing the same way.

In the problems below, circle the shape that is *congruent* to the colored one on the far left. When you are done, add up the numbers in the circled shapes to figure out the number of trees that are saved for every ton (2,000 pounds or 907 kilograms) of recycled paper.

Add up the circled numbers. How many trees are saved for every ton of recycled paper? ________

Journal

Use a blank sheet of paper if you need more space.

Take a look inside your refrigerator. What do you see? Write a story from the point of view of one of the objects in the refrigerator. Describe what your day is like.

How's The Weather?

Do Temperatures Vary Around The World?

Celeste, Vega and Tripp want to learn more about the countries that their volunteers have come from. One thing they've researched is the average temperature in each of the cities for the month of July.

Below you will see the name of the city and the average temperature in degrees Fahrenheit. Fill in the thermometer to show the temperature of each city.

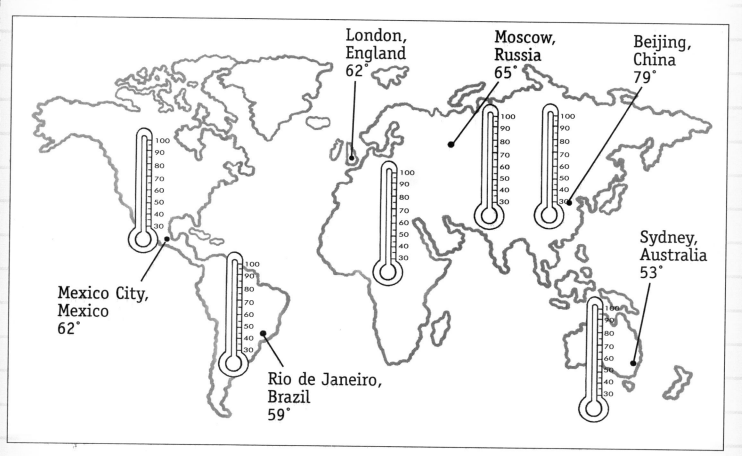

In Rio de Janeiro and Sydney, it's winter in July. How do the temperatures in these cities compare to the others?

_____

Why is it warmer in Beijing than in Moscow?

_____

Math Quiz

1. Which number is the same as $\frac{97}{100}$?

   a. .0097   b. .97

   c. 97   d. 9.7

2. What number should n equal in the math problem below?

   n + 22 = 196

   a. 174   b. 176   c. 178

3. Take the number 15,229 and increase the value of the digit in the thousands place by 4. What is the new number?

   a. 15,729   b. 55,229   c. 19,229

4. What is another way to write 4 + 4 + 4 + 4 ?

   a. 44 + 44   b. 4 + 4
   c. 4 x 4   d. 4 x 2

5. Which of these numbers would equal 7,000 if it were rounded to the nearest thousands place?

   a. 6,483   b. 7,622
   c. 7,114   d. 6,298

6. What number should n equal in the math problem below?

   n – 14 = 673

   a. 687   b. 659
   c. 649   d. 688

weird science

Flies have eyes that are made up of hundreds of smaller eyes. Eckhhh!

150

Math Games

Each shape has a value. Scales 1 and 2 are in perfect balance.
How many squares are needed to balance scales 3, 4, 5, 6 and 7?

■ =12   ▲ =9   ● =1

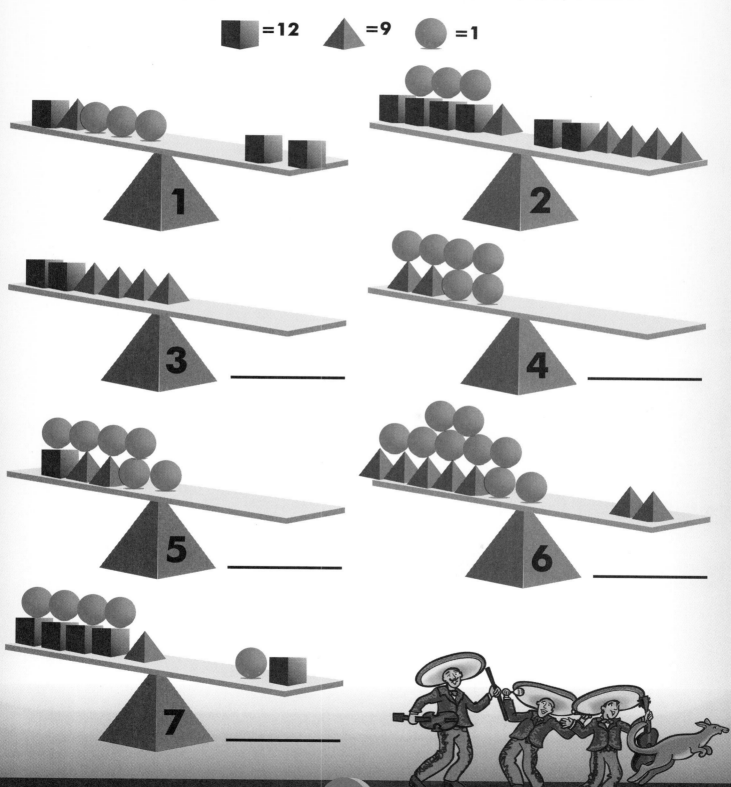

Wanted: Volunteers

Chapter 11

The group's final stop was the local library. Quietly, they looked for Mr. Mwanja, their favorite librarian.

At the side door, the children could see Mr. Mwanja on his break. He was sitting on a bench in the sunshine, and his back was to them. The children walked outside. Tripp was about to speak when Vega waved at him to be quiet. He looked where she was pointing.

There was an odd pile of curled wood shavings at Mr. Mwanja's feet. Mr. Mwanja was carving a piece of wood between his knees. Only when Vega cleared her throat did he look up.

"What a wonderful surprise. What can I do for three of my favorite readers?" Mr. Mwanja was used to the children's visits to the library.

Vega was so interested in his carving that she forgot to be polite. "What are you working on?" she asked.

"Today—a giraffe." Mr. Mwanja held up his work. Half of it looked like a giraffe. The other half was still rough and uncarved.

"Where did you learn to do that?" asked Tripp.

"I have been carving for a long time. Carving is a tradition in my land. Even long ago they made statues of the animals and people in Africa, to show respect and to honor them." Mr. Mwanja looked at the form in his hands.

"Would you give a demonstration at the Community Center?" asked Celeste.

"To teach people how to make little piles of curly wood shavings? Who would want to learn that?"

Tripp jumped in. "Your carving is really great, Mr. Mwanja. Won't you consider it? Please?"

Mr. Mwanja looked doubtful, but after he thought about it, he agreed.

Chapter 11

Skill: Sequence of Events

Number these events in the order in which they occurred in Chapter 11. Label the items 1 (first) through 8 (last).

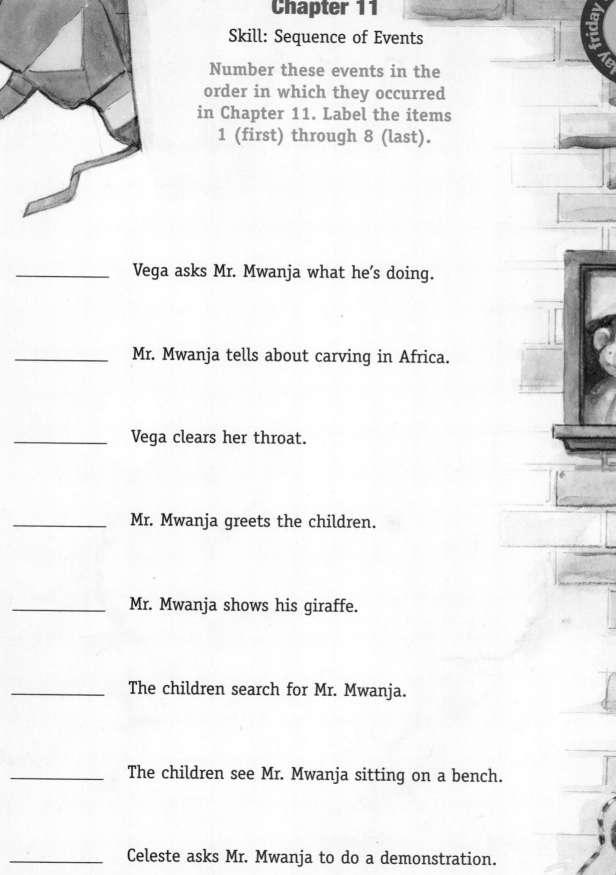

_____ Vega asks Mr. Mwanja what he's doing.

_____ Mr. Mwanja tells about carving in Africa.

_____ Vega clears her throat.

_____ Mr. Mwanja greets the children.

_____ Mr. Mwanja shows his giraffe.

_____ The children search for Mr. Mwanja.

_____ The children see Mr. Mwanja sitting on a bench.

_____ Celeste asks Mr. Mwanja to do a demonstration.

Add some ADVERBS?

If an adjective describes a noun, what describes a verb? Adverbs! They not only describe verbs but also other adjectives and even other adverbs.

What are some other adverbs? Look at the sentences below:

Ms. Darcy **quietly** opened her door. (How did she open the door?)

Vega **often** has cereal for breakfast. (How frequently does she eat cereal?)

Adverbs answer how, when, where, and why. They sometimes end in "ly" like "quietly," "softly," "merrily," and "quickly." Sometimes, they do not, like in the case of "often" and "late."

Make 'Em Funny!

Adverbs can totally change the meaning of a sentence. Circle the adverbs in the sentences below and replace each of them with another adverb that will make the sentence funny or goofy. You can be as silly as you want to be.

1. Tripp carefully walked around the very big dog today.
My funny version:

2. Soon, Vega quickly saw how to solve the math problem.
My funny version:

3. Celeste spoke very quietly in the library yesterday.
My funny version:

4. Peter immediately pulled a stack of extremely lovely photos from his bag
My funny version:

OUT ⇗

IN ⇗

Prefixes

Prefixes appear at the beginning of words and they change their meaning.

Prefix	Means
un	not
mis	wrong
re	again
pre	before

Use the correct prefix to write the word that matches each definition below.

1. write it again _____

2. said wrong thing _____

3. do again _____

4. pay in advance _____

Abbreviations

Abbreviations are shortened versions of written words.

Write the correct abbreviations for the words below:

Example: *Mister*   →   *Mr.*

1. Doctor _____

2. Road _____

3. Street _____

4. United States of America _____

5. Junior _____

6. Sunday _____

7. Post Office _____

8. Boulevard _____

9. Senior _____

10. Company _____

11. Wednesday _____

12. September _____

Journal

Use a blank sheet of paper if you need more space.

I'm thankful today because...

_____

_____

_____

_____

_____

_____

_____

_____

_____

_____

_____

_____

_____

_____

_____

_____

_____

_____

_____

Wanted: Volunteers

Chapter 12

Tonight was the night. Vega and Celeste couldn't believe how many people came to the Community Center. Many wore traditional costumes to show off their family's history. The hum of voices talking and laughing charged the room with an energy that had long been missing from the Center.

The girls viewed the mural Celeste had painted for the occasion. They were surprised that Tripp was late.

"Tripp will just have to catch up," said Celeste. "Orientation is about to start."

Ms. Darcy began by introducing the new volunteers. When she got to Mrs. Radanovich, she announced that someone very special would be introducing her. Celeste and Vega were surprised to see Tripp walking to the microphone in a suit and tie. Slowly, he began.

"Mrs. Radanovich is from Russia. She will be sharing with you a special collection of dolls. But her collection is incomplete. Mrs. Radanovich, I have someone here who can help."

A very old woman made her way to the center stage. In her hand she carried a doll no bigger than a thimble.

The girls immediately guessed that Tripp's surprise was to bring Mrs. Radanovich's sister to Springville. They later discovered that Tripp's uncle, a pilot, had made the flight arrangements for Mrs. Radanovich's sister. The day Tripp had to go home from Vega's house was the day the sister had arrived.

Later, Ms. Darcy motioned the children toward the front door. "This will just take a minute. Do you think this is the best place?" She held a bulletin board against the wall.

Vega, Tripp and Celeste stared. A banner across the bulletin board read "Volunteer of the Month." Their pictures were on the front with the caption "A Three-Way Tie."

Ms. Darcy hugged the children. "I am so proud of you. You have used your time to help your community. And you put some life back in the Center."

"Thanks, Ms. Darcy," chimed Vega, Tripp and Celeste.

The music started, and the three volunteers made their way to the gym. Was it just their imagination, or was everyone glowing with pride tonight?

Chapter 12

Skill: Reading Comprehension

Answer the questions below on the lines provided.

1. Where does the action in Chapter 12 take place?

_____

2. What special contribution did Celeste make to the Center?

_____

3. What is special about Mrs. Radanovich's introduction?

_____

4. Who is the surprise visitor?

_____

5. How did the surprise visitor get to Springville?

_____

6. What does Ms. Darcy need help with?

_____

7. What does the top banner on the bulletin board say?

_____

8. Whose pictures are on the bulletin board?

_____

9. Why is Ms. Darcy proud of the three children?

_____

Adult supervision may be required.

Bugs!

Creepy crawlies? Slimy and gross? No way! There are more than 800,000 different kinds of insects out there. There are so many, in fact, that scientists haven't even discovered them all yet!

This makes insects one of the more interesting animals to study. An insect is any bug that has six legs and three body parts: a head, thorax and abdomen.

Would you like to be an entomologist (en-toe-mall-o-just) for a day? An entomologist is a person who studies insects. You can learn a lot about insects through observation, that is, watching carefully and noticing details.

What you need:

- plastic or glass container with lid
- insect guide (you can get one from the library)
- pencil
- paper
- magnifying lens (optional)

What to do:

1) Poke holes in the lid of your container so the insect will have air.

2) Go outside and search for bugs! Try looking under rocks, logs, or other hiding places.

3) When you find one you like, carefully scoop it into your container. Include things you find near the insect like dirt, twigs, or leaves.

4) Find a quiet place where you can observe the insect. Be careful not to hurt or kill the insect.

5) For 10 minutes, try to notice everything you can about the insect by watching it carefully. Use the magnifying lens to see the insect better, but make sure you do this in the shade.

6) You can try drawing the insect. Make a list of your observations. Here are some things you may want to look for: colors, number of legs, wings, sounds, how it moves, eyes, mouth parts, and number of antennae.

What it does:

- Once you have all your observations, you can look up the insect in your guide. What other information can you find?

- When you have learned all about this insect, take it back to where you found it! Empty your container and find a new bug.

Remember to use the Scientific Method!

1) Make your hypothesis.

2) Record your observations.

3) Draw your conclusions.

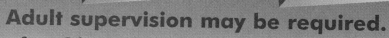

Adult supervision may be required.

Static Electric Circus

You can make paper jump into the air like magic with science! You've heard the phrase "opposites attract"? Well, now you can see for yourself.

What you need:

- small plastic comb
- paper torn into little bits
- wool cloth
- a balloon

What to do:

1) Lay the bits of paper out on a table top.

2) Rub the plastic comb back and forth on the cloth very quickly.

3) Slowly bring the comb close to the papers without touching them.

What's happening:

- When you rub the comb, you give it a positive electrical charge.

- The bits of paper do not have a charge, and are attracted to the comb.

- You might notice some bits of paper flying off the comb. This happens because once the paper touches the comb, it can get the same charge as the comb. The two objects, both with positive or negative charges, will repel one another, but two objects with different charges will be attracted to one another.

Try this:

1) You can observe the same static electric charge by rubbing an inflated balloon on your hair.

2) Try this in front of the mirror. What does the hair do once you have given the balloon a charge?

3) Rub some more. Now see if the balloon will stick to a wall.

4) What other things can you attract with your charged balloon?

Remember to use the Scientific Method!

1) Make your hypothesis.

2) Record your observations.

3) Draw your conclusions.

Adult supervision may be required.

Eggstraordinary Science! – Part I

What would you say if someone told you they could bounce an egg? You'd probably think of poor old Humpty Dumpty, right? Well, with a little chemistry on your side, you really can bounce an egg.

What you need:

- a raw egg, with shell
- a cup
- vinegar

What to do:

1) Place the egg inside the cup.

2) Pour vinegar over the egg until it is completely covered.

3) Observe for a few minutes. What do you notice?

4) Wait 24 hours.

5) Check the egg the next day.

6) Make as many observations as you can: touch, smell, and look at the egg. How is it different than when you first put it in? You might want to get out another raw egg so you can make a good comparison.

7) Take out the egg. What is left inside the cup? Try bouncing the egg. Pretty neat!

What's happening:

- When you first put the vinegar in with the egg you probably noticed some bubbles coming off the eggshell.

- These bubbles were caused by a chemical reaction between the eggshell and the vinegar. The vinegar dissolved the eggshell.

- The white material left in the cup is dissolved eggshell. It has been through a chemical change. There is no way to get back the original eggshell.

- The vinegar chemically reacted with the rest of the egg, causing it to become solid and rubbery enough to bounce.

Remember to use the Scientific Method!

1) Make your hypothesis.

2) Record your observations.

3) Draw your conclusions.

Adult supervision may be required.

Eggstraordinary Science! - Part II

Have you ever seen a ship in a bottle? Well, you are going to try to get an egg into a bottle without even touching it! This is an amazing trick that will impress just about anybody! **You must have an adult to help you with the eggsperiment.**

What you need:

- a small hard-boiled egg
- matches
- a 3-inch (8 cm) by 3-inch (8 cm) piece of paper
- vegetable oil
- an empty, clean, wide-mouthed GLASS container (apple juice jug works well)

What to do:

1) Peel and rinse the hard-boiled egg. Have it ready to go.

2) Take a teaspoon of vegetable oil and rub it around the mouth of the container.

3) An adult must light a match. Have an adult set fire to the paper, and drop it quickly down into the jar while placing the egg on top.

4) Stand back and observe!

5) It may take a few tries to get it right!

What's happening:

- The burning paper warms up the air molecules inside the jar. They expand and squeeze their way OUT of the jar, past the egg. You may have noticed the egg "hopping" on top of the jar. This was the molecules pushing their way out.

- Most of the air molecules leave the inside of the bottle, making a low pressure zone.

- The air OUTSIDE the bottle is a high pressure zone.

- High pressure zones like to push their way into low pressure zones. So the air molecules on the outside of the bottle started pushing on the egg to get into the bottle! They push so hard, the egg has no choice but to go along with them!

Remember to use the Scientific Method!

1) Make your hypothesis.

2) Record your observations.

3) Draw your conclusions.

Adult supervision may be required.

Magic Markers

Is a black marker just a black marker? Is green just green? Actually, the colors in markers are sometimes made of other colors mixed together. You can test this for yourself in this colorful experiment.

What you need:

- a set of markers
- water
- a cup or mug
- scissors
- long pencils or pens
- a coffee filter
- tape
- paper and pencil
- ruler

What to do:

1) Cut the coffee filter into a 1/2 inch (1 cm) by 7 inch (18 cm) strip.

2) Choose three different colored markers and put three different dots horizontally along the paper, about 3 inches (8 cm) from the bottom.

3) Put one of the long pencils or pens in the cup.

4) Tape the end of the coffee filter to the end of the pen that is sticking up out of the cup.

5) Carefully fill the cup with water so just the bottom of the filter paper gets wet.

6) Observe what happens as the water spreads up the filter paper.

7) Record what combinations of colors make the single marker color.

What's happening:

As the water spreads through the dot you made with the marker, it separates the colors out of the marker in a beautiful display. You can test all of your markers!

- Which markers are made of the most colors? The fewest?
- How do the colors change as time passes?
- Can you still see the original color you started with?
- Does this work with all markers? See if you can find a permanent marker or highlighter to test.

Remember to use the Scientific Method!

1) Make your hypothesis.

2) Record your observations.

3) Draw your conclusions.

Adult supervision may be required.

There's Air in There

Air is everywhere. You can't see it, you don't usually feel it, most of the time you probably don't even think about it. So how do you know it's there? Here is an experiment that wouldn't be possible without the air!

What you need:

- a cup
- a bowl
- water
- paper

What to do:

1) Fill the bowl about halfway with water.

2) Crumple up a piece of paper and stuff it down into the cup so that it is stuck to the bottom of the cup.

3) Turn the cup upside down.

4) Carefully place the cup straight down into the water.

5) Will the paper be wet or dry when you take out the cup?

6) Check the paper by bringing the cup straight up out of the bowl.

Why it's dry:

The paper stays dry inside the underwater cup because there's air in there!

- There is air inside the cup along with the paper.

- When you put the cup down inside the water, the air stays inside the cup. Air takes up room.

- Since the air is taking up all the space inside the cup there's not enough room for the water to come in. As a result, the paper stays dry!

- What would you have to do to get the paper wet? Where does the air go?

Remember to use the Scientific Method!

1) Make your hypothesis.

2) Record your observations.

3) Draw your conclusions.

Volcanoes:
Research!

Adult supervision is recommended.

Introduction to the Project

The research opportunity presented by this project will help your child discover this geological process and its effects on the surrounding environment. Your child will have the opportunity to make a papier-mâché model of a volcano and conduct various volcano-related experiments. These processes will help your child practice following directions and using his or her scientific observation and experimentation skills.

You may want to supervise your child throughout the project. You can help him or her with the papier-mâché process because using the right consistency of paste is important to the success of the models and experiments.

Master Materials List

old newspapers

water

1 $\frac{1}{2}$ c. (354.9 ml) flour

$\frac{1}{2}$ c. (118.3 ml) sugar

masking tape

saucepan

3 large sheets of cardboard or plywood, or 3 foil trays, at least 24 in. × 16 in. (60.9 cm × 40.6 cm)

non-water-based craft paints in white, brown, black, and green

4 medium-size paintbrushes or disposable foam applicators

paper towels or rags for clean-up

2-liter plastic soda bottle

5 raisins or other dried fruit

shallow cardboard box

scissors

damp dirt or sand

pen or pencil

2 foam or plastic plates

2 foam or plastic cups

2 plastic straws

$\frac{3}{4}$ c. (177.4 ml) water, milk, or juice

$\frac{3}{4}$ c. (177.4 ml) honey, vegetable oil, or corn syrup

plastic or paper cup, or an empty film cylinder

1 T. (14.8 ml) + 1 $\frac{1}{2}$ tsp. (4.9 ml) baking soda

$\frac{1}{4}$ c. (59.1 ml) + 2 T. (29.6 ml) vinegar

Directions

1. To begin learning about volcanoes, read about them from sources at the library or from an encyclopedia at home. You also can use web sites such as www.volcanoworld.org

2. Find out about the three types of volcanoes. What are some similarities among the types? What are some differences? Write notes in the chart below.

Beneath the Earth's land and water is a thin layer of rocky material called the Earth's *crust.* Hot, melted rock, or *magma,* can travel up from the center of Earth and burst through holes and cracks in the crust. This is how a *volcano* forms. *Active* volcanoes are those that erupt fairly often. Earth has more than 1,500 active volcanoes!

Volcanoes are found on land and under oceans all over the world. Volcanoes are grouped by shape and by the way they erupt. There are three types of volcanoes: composite, or *stratovolcano*; cinder cone; and shield.

Types of Volcanoes	Similarities	Differences
Composite/ Stratovolcano		
Cinder Cone		
Shield		

Volcanoes:

Composite Volcano, Step 1

Adult supervision is recommended.

Materials

old newspapers
4 c. (946.4 ml) water
   (2 c. [473.2 ml] cold;
   2 c. [473.2 ml] boiling)
$\frac{1}{2}$ c. (118.3 ml) flour
3 T. (44.4 ml) sugar
saucepan
masking tape
large sheet of cardboard
   or plywood, or a foil tray,
   at least 24 in. × 16 in.
   (60.9 cm × 40.6 cm)

Composite volcanoes are the most common type of volcano in the world. They are built in layers by multiple eruptions. Most composite volcano eruptions begin with clouds of ash, which are created by gases in the magma. The gases escape so forcefully that they blast rock into billions of little pieces. As the eruption continues, the ash is replaced by *lava,* or magma that has broken through Earth's surface. The resulting composite volcano is made up of many layers of ash and lava.

Directions

1. Tear about 15 sheets of newspaper into 2-in. (5.1-cm) strips. Soak the strips in warm water.

2. Prepare the paste. Mix the flour with 2 c. (473.2 ml) of cold water in a bowl.

3. With an adult's help, boil 2 c. (473.2 ml) of water in a saucepan.

4. Add the flour mixture to the boiling water. Return to a boil.

5. Remove from heat and add the sugar.

6. Let this mixture cool for at least a half hour; it will thicken as it cools.

7. Ball up about fifteen pieces of newspaper (not the newspaper strips; they are still soaking). Pile them to form a tall cone shape with steep sides on the cardboard or plywood. An uneven, "bumpy" form will make a more realistic volcano. Hold the cone together loosely with a few pieces of masking tape. Keep a small opening at the top for the volcano's crater, or *vent.* Make sure the opening is large enough for a small plastic or paper cup or an empty film cylinder.

8. Remove the newspaper strips from the water one at a time. Drain excess water from each strip.

9. Dip one strip into the paste. Overlap it vertically on the volcano from the top to the bottom. Run the top edge of the strip over the rim of the vent and tuck it into the opening.

10. Repeat steps 8 and 9, overlapping the remaining strips vertically around the form.

11. Set the volcano form in a place where it can dry thoroughly for one to two days. Cover the paste and keep it in the refrigerator until you are ready for the next layer.

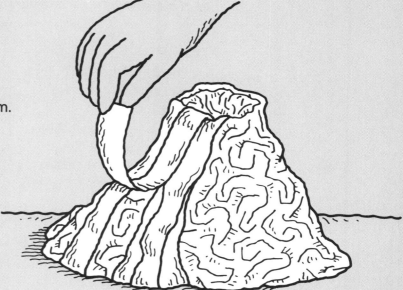

12. After the first layer has dried, prepare to add a second layer of newspaper strips to your model. Tear 15 more newspaper pages into strips. Soak the strips in warm water.

13. Repeat steps 8 and 9 until you have added an entirely new layer of newspaper strips.

14. Set your volcano in a safe place, and allow the second layer to dry thoroughly for another one to two days.

Extension

There are six types of volcanic eruptions—Plinian, Vulcanian, Hawaiian, Icelandic, Strombolian, and Peleean. At the library, read about these eruptions. Then, on the lines below, write the eruptions in order from least explosive eruption to most explosive eruption.

_____

_____

_____

_____

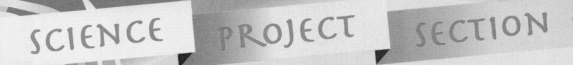

Volcanoes:
Composite Volcano, Step 2
Adult supervision is recommended.

Materials
non-water-based craft
   paints in white, brown
   and black
medium-size paintbrushes
   or disposable foam
   applicators (one brush
   for each color, if possible)
paper towels or rags
   for cleanup

Directions

1. Review your research
   about composite
   volcanoes. Refer to
   photographs of composite
   volcanoes such as Mount Saint
   Helens as you paint your model.

2. Paint your composite volcano model. You might want to
   paint your volcano different shades of brown and black.

3. Because stratovolcanoes are so tall, many are topped with
   layers of ice and snow. Use white paint to add snow and ice
   to the top of your volcano.

4. Set the volcano aside for 24 hours to dry thoroughly.

Dormant volcanoes are those that have
been quiet for a long time, maybe even
for centuries. However, they still show
signs of erupting again. These signs may
include rising steam or lava bubbling in
the volcano's crater. If a volcano hasn't
shown signs of activity for a very long
time, it is known as *extinct.*

Mount Saint Helens, a stratovolcano
in Washington, erupted in 1980—for
the first time in over 120 years! The
explosion lasted nine hours and ejected
millions of tons of ash 15 mi. (24.1 km)
into the air.

Volcanoes:
Volcanic Eruption!
Adult supervision is recommended.

Materials
one of your
    volcano models
plastic or paper cup,
    empty film cylinder
1 T. (14.8 ml) baking soda
2 T. (29.6 ml) vinegar

Volcanoes have fascinated human beings for ages. They are one of the most powerful forces in nature. You have built a model to represent a volcano. Now you have the opportunity to use your volcano to make your very own volcanic eruption.

Directions
1. Gather your supplies, and either take them outside or set them in a large sink inside your house.
2. Place the cup or cylinder in the volcano's vent.
3. Spoon the baking soda into the container.
4. Pour the vinegar into the baking soda. Watch your volcano erupt!

Congratulations! You have learned many important facts about volcanoes, including how they form and what comes out of them. You also have built a model of a volcano, and you have made your very own volcanic eruption. As you begin fourth grade, you will have many interesting facts about volcanoes to share with your classmates.

Answers

MONDAY
PAGE 5
CROSSWORD

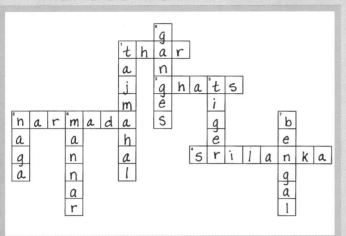

TUESDAY
PAGE 6
ADDITION AND SUBTRACTION REGROUPING

1. 77-68 = 9
2. 39+39 = 78
3. 84-27 = 57
4. 99+12 = 111
5. 63-59 = 4
6. 23+67 = 90
7. 52-18 = 34
8. 45+56 = 101
9. 100-46 = 54

PAGE 7
MATH RIDDLES

A. 970
D. 474
S. 743
L. 753
C. 960
E. 257
R. 619
P. 588
O. 937
F. 905
I. 837
K. 926

Answer: Pickles

WEDNESDAY
PAGE 9
SINK OR FLOAT?

THURSDAY
PAGE 10
MATCHING EQUATIONS

1. C   3. A   5. C   7. D
2. B   4. D   6. B   8. A

PAGE 11
MATH GAMES

Numbers are added to each circled number in a sequence.

1. 16 The sequence is 3, 4, 5, 6.
2. 35 The sequence is 11, 12, 13, 14.
3. 19 The sequence is 3, 4, 5, 6.
4. 13 The sequence is subtract 4.
5. 48 The sequence is subtract 8.
6. 39 The sequence is add 6.

WEEK ONE
FRIDAY

PAGE 13

WORD SEARCH

flyer
ice cream
sketch
carrier
friends
ideas
exhibit
tag
summer
pickles

I	C	E	C	R	E	A	M				F
											L
E		S	U	M	M	E	R		Y		
	X						E				
	H					R		S			
P	F	R	I	E	N	D	S		K	C	G
	I		B				I	D	E	A	S
	C		I				T		R		
	K		T				C		R		
			L				H		I		
			E						E		
			S						R		

CHALLENGE

(Possible answers)
1. sneaker, sandal, flip-flop, slipper
2. maple, pine, oak, birch
3. lane, track, highway, Pearl Street, 4th Avenue

SATURDAY

PAGE 14

FIX THE FACTS

1. E   4. B
2. D   5. A
3. F   6. C

PAGE 15

NAME THE SENTENCE TYPE

1. Question   4. Statement
2. Statement   5. Question
3. Command   6. Command

MAZE

SUNDAY

PAGE 16

COMPLETE THE ANALOGIES

1. cake   3. hand   5. grape juice   7. kitten   9. land
2. playground   4. radio   6. seed   8. milk   10. frog

WEEK TWO
MONDAY

PAGE 19

CROSSWORD

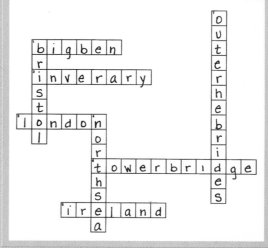

TUESDAY

PAGE 20

ADD UP AND ROUND UP!

1. 597
2. 885
3. 313
4. 201
5. 910
6. 545

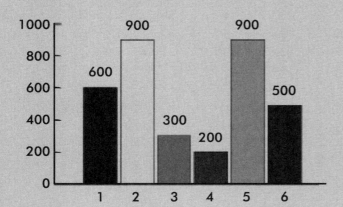

PAGE 21

LOCK BOX MYSTERY!

1. 4, 15, 26, 37
2. add 11 to previous number
3. 9, 20, 31, 42
4. 13, 24, 35, 46
5. 6, 17, 28, 39

UNITED KINGDOM

WEDNESDAY

PAGE 23

MIX FOR KICKS!

1. Sugar – solution
2. Sand – mixture
3. Salt – solution
4. Baking Soda – solution
5. Pepper – mixture

THURSDAY

PAGE 24

PLACE VALUE

1. 682,405
2. 996,827
3. 70,511
4. 300,014
5. 304,122
6. 97,061
7. 532,709

PAGE 25

MATH GAMES

3. 9 triangles
4. 4 triangles
5. 3 triangles
6. 6 triangles
7. 5 triangles

FRIDAY

PAGE 27

VOCABULARY

1. B
2. C
3. B
4. A
5. D
6. C
7. A

SATURDAY

PAGE 28

WEIRD VERBS

flew · read · made
wrote · stood · slept
ate · drew · sang

PAGE 29

COMPOUND WORDS

bedtime · horsefly
sunlight · nightlight
horseback · moonshine

MAZE

OUT

IN

S			D					W		E		L		F
	L	R	E			D		R		O		E		S
		E	W		P	O	O	T		T		A		
R	E	A	D			O	T	S			N			
R	E	A	D			O	T	S						
A						S		G						
D														
								E		D		A		M

SUNDAY

PAGE 30

FISHING FOR SYNONYMS

Harmful – Dangerous · Big – Large
Run – Sprint · Angry – Furious
Cheerful – Happy · Professor – Teacher
Physician – Doctor · Frightening – Scary
Hairy – Furry

MONDAY

PAGE 33

CROSSWORD

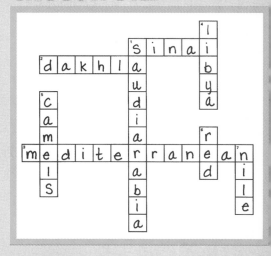

TUESDAY

PAGE 34

FRACTION COMPARISONS

1. $\dfrac{2}{5}$ = $\dfrac{4}{10}$

2. $\dfrac{5}{12}$ < $\dfrac{6}{8}$

3. $\dfrac{12}{16}$ > $\dfrac{4}{8}$

4. $\dfrac{11}{16}$ > $\dfrac{3}{16}$

5. $\dfrac{1}{4}$ < $\dfrac{4}{8}$

6. $\dfrac{8}{12}$ = $\dfrac{4}{6}$

PAGE 35

PIZZA PARTY!

1. $\dfrac{4}{10}$ 4. $\dfrac{6}{10}$

2. $\dfrac{8}{10}$ 5. $\dfrac{1}{10}$

3. $\dfrac{5}{10}$ 6. $\dfrac{2}{10}$

WEEK THREE
WEDNESDAY
PAGE 37
HOME IN THE BIOME!

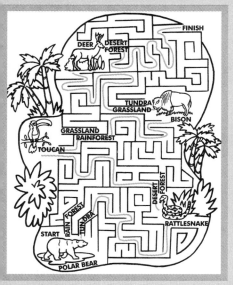

THURSDAY

PAGE 38
FRACTIONS AS DECIMALS

1. e   4. c   7. d   10. e
2. a   5. d   8. a
3. b   6. c   9. b

PAGE 39
MATH GAMES

1. 21   3. 44
2. 37   4. 28

FRIDAY
PAGE 41
READING COMPREHENSION

1. In Pauline Darcy's office

2. The director of the Community Center

3. Helpful

4. Volunteers

5. Budget cuts force volunteers to bring their own supplies.

6. Volunteers can't afford to bring their own supplies.

7. They must find a way to get volunteers and to get the volunteers to bring their own supplies.

8. Tripp has his own great idea.

SATURDAY

PAGE 42
NOUN SCAVENGER HUNT!

Community Center Offers Summer Classes

Due to budget cuts, the Springville Community Center will no longer receive money to hire instructors to teach summer classes. Center organizers say they will still offer summer classes and are asking for volunteers with skills to share to submit ideas for class subjects.

Volunteers should have knowledge, energy, time, and be able to provide things that will help the class learn, such as food, music, or photos. The Center has walls to display art and space for museum displays.

PAGE 43
MAZE

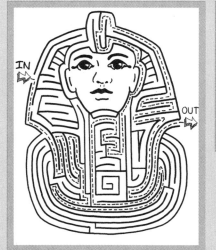

FUN WITH PHONICS

	A					C						
H		C				C	H	O	R	U	S	C
E			H				R		E			H
A				E		C	E	O				R
D					H	N	B		M			I
A	S				O	I	A			E	S	S
C	T				R		C					T
H	O			O	D		K					M
E	M		L				A					A
	A	H					C					S
	C	C					H					
C	H	R	Y	S	A	N	T	H	E	M	U	M

stomach   chrysanthemum
chrome   chlorine
ache   chorus
headache   chord
backache   Christmas

		¹l		
⁴v	e	n	i	c	e

Crossword answers:
- Venice
- Vatican
- Liguria
- adriatica
- Capri
- austria
- Salerno
- Sicily
- ionian

THURSDAY

PAGE 52

COMPARING NUMBERS

1. <   4. <   7. <
2. <   5. >   8. >
3. >   6. >   9. >

PAGE 53

MATH GAMES

Numbers are subtracted from each circled number in sequence.

1. 6 - The sequence is subtract 5, 4, 3, 2.
2. 18 - The sequence is subtract 6, 5, 4, 3.
3. 10 - The sequence is subtract 9, 8, 7, 6.
4. 16 - The sequence is subtract 10, 9, 8, 7.
5. 24 - The sequence is subtract 6, 5, 4, 3.
6. 7 - The sequence is subtract 8, 7, 6, 5.

FRIDAY

PAGE 55

SEQUENCE OF EVENTS

2, 7, 6, 1, 8, 4, 3, 5

SATURDAY

PAGE 56

CRAZY CAPERS

Tony

MAZE   PAGE 57

PLURAL ENDINGS

1. boxes   5. teeth
2. mice   6. beaches
3. flowers   7. countries
4. leaves   8. dishes

SUNDAY

PAGE 58

FISHING FOR ANTONYMS

Early – Late   Nervous – Relaxed
Huge – Tiny   Morning – Night
Dangerous – Safe   Long – Short
Black – White   East – West
Love – Hate

ITALY

CROSSWORD

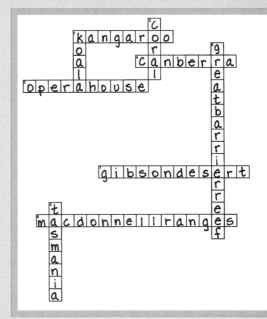

TUESDAY

FRACTION EQUATIONS

1. 1 OR $\frac{2}{2}$

2. $\frac{2}{8}$ OR $\frac{1}{4}$

3. $\frac{12}{10}$ OR $1\frac{1}{5}$

4. $\frac{11}{7}$ OR $1\frac{4}{7}$

5. $\frac{4}{6}$ OR $\frac{2}{3}$

6. $\frac{1}{4}$

7. $\frac{12}{9}$ OR $1\frac{1}{3}$

8. 1 OR $\frac{6}{6}$

EXCELLENT EQUIVALENTS!

1. $\frac{2}{4} = \frac{1}{2}, \frac{3}{6}$ OR $\frac{4}{8}$

2. $\frac{3}{4} = \frac{6}{8}$

3. $\frac{4}{6} = \frac{2}{3}$

4. $\frac{1}{3} = \frac{2}{6}$

5. $\frac{2}{8} = \frac{1}{4}$

WEDNESDAY

FOOD!

1. Celery – stem E
2. Carrot – root P
3. Lettuce – leaves R
4. Spinach – leaves S
5. Radish – root O

answer: Spore

THURSDAY

ROUNDING

1. 80
2. 10
3. 20
4. 70
5. 60
6. 50
7. 50
8. 40
9. 20
10. 40
11. 60
12. 80
13. 90
14. 70

MATH GAMES

3. 3 Circles
4. 2 Circles
5. 3 Circles
6. 3 Circles
7. 2 Circles

DETERMINE CAUSE AND EFFECT

Dmitri's mother and grandmother taught him to cook. — Dmitri is a good cook.

The smells from the café kitchen were good. — Tripp's mouth watered.

Baklava has lots of honey in it. — Celeste has to lick her fingers.

Dmitri says that his mother is an expert cook. — Dmitri volunteers his mother to lead a cooking class.

The children ate their lunches. — The children's food "disappeared."

Dmitri has to run his café. — Dmitri cannot volunteer at the Center.

SATURDAY

PAGE 70
FIX THE FACTS

1. A	4. E
2. C	5. B
3. D	6. F

PAGE 71
MAZE

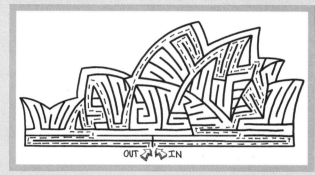

OUT ← → IN

POSSESSIVE NOUNS

1. sailors'
2. waiter's
3. teacher's
4. kids'
5. lifeguards'
6. actors'

SUNDAY

PAGE 72
PAST TENSE VERBS

1. stopped	4. sang, sung	7. ran	10. drove	13. threw
2. blew	5. cooked	8. grew	11. ate	14. made
3. told	6. watched	9. came	12. took	15. gave

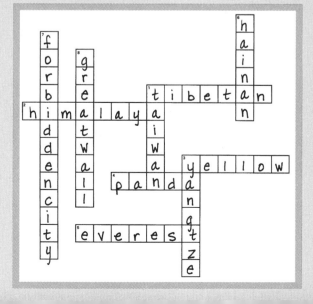

TUESDAY

PAGE 76

MULTIPLICATION & DIVISION

1. 72
2. 9
3. 36
4. 6
5. 100
6. 8
7. 9
8. 45

PAGE 77

SEARCH AND SEEK!

1. 49
2. 8
3. 24
4. 42
5. 6
6. 5
7. 18
8. 28
9. 4
10. 9

Answer: Volunteers

WEDNESDAY

PAGE 79

FOOD GROUPS

1. Cheese Pizza – vegetable, bread & cereal, milk   E, P, O
2. Turkey Sandwich – bread & cereal, meat   P, E
3. Bowl of Cereal with Milk – bread & cereal, milk   P, N
4. Yogurt with Strawberries – milk, fruit   I, R

Guess Who I Am! PEPPERONI

THURSDAY

PAGE 80

STORY PROBLEMS

1. $5,600.00
2. $1,200.00
3. $6,800.00

PAGE 81

MATH GAMES

The left and right numbers are added and then multiplied by the bottom number.

1. 12 2. 49 3. 0 4. 24

FRIDAY

PAGE 83

VERBS

know	tell	come					
		wait	nod				
			follow	lead	return	am	
						say	
see	smile	give		share	make	add	
live		help	learn	have			
wave					greet	stop	talk
visit	put	breathe	show	enter	explain		run

SATURDAY

TOTALLY WEIRD PLURALS!

goose – geese

ox – oxen

tooth – teeth

deer – deer

person – people

mouse – mice

man – men

child – children

foot – feet

sheep – sheep

moose – moose

platypus – platypuses or platypi

MAZE

CHINA

POSSESSIVE PRONOUNS

1. Its dish is too full.
2. That toy is hers.
3. That cat is ours.
4. Those shoes are his.

SUNDAY

FISHING FOR HOMONYMS

Where – Wear

Bear – Bare

Inn – In

Blew – Blue

Beat – Beet

Two – Too

Coral – Choral

Aunt – Ant

Meet – Meat

WEEK SEVEN
MONDAY

CROSSWORD

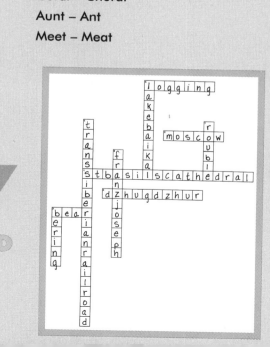

WEEK SEVEN

TUESDAY

PAGE 90

ADDITION AND SUBTRACTION WITH DECIMALS

1. 1.738
2. .412
3. .001
4. 1.419
5. .412
6. 1.120
7. .962
8. .231

PAGE 91

LINE 'EM UP!

1. 3.90
2. 1.40
3. 0.77
4. 1.09
5. 0.88
6. 3.36
7. 2.66
8. 2.98
9. 1.65
10. 3.15

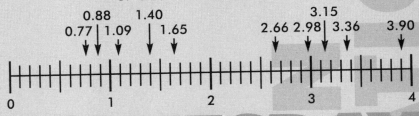

WEDNESDAY

PAGE 93

PEOPLE EVERYWHERE!

Over 1 billion – China, India S, S

<60,000,000 – Australia, Italy C, N

Most – China U

Least – Australia E

What Am I ? CENSUS

THURSDAY

PAGE 94

NUMBER LINES

1. 71
2. 203
3. -3
4. 0
5. 1.1
6. 1.37

PAGE 95

MATH GAMES

Multiply by 2.

1. 24
2. 40
3. 28
4. 12
5. 18
6. 32

VOCABULARY

1. C
2. A
3. B
4. D
5. C
6. B
7. A
8. C

FRIDAY

PAGE 97

SATURDAY

PAGE 98

FIX THE FACTS

1. D
2. C
3. E
4. A
5. B
6. F

CORRECT THE SENTENCES

1. Where are you going on vacation, Sally?

2. We are going to my grandma's cottage in Minnesota.

3. I've heard it gets really, really cold in Minnesota.

4. It is cold in the winter, but the summers are warm.

PAGE 99

MAZE

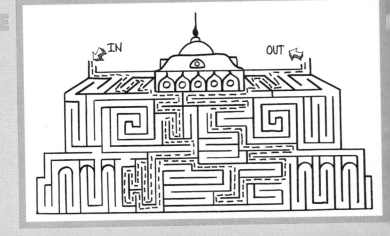

RUSSIAN FEDERATION

SUNDAY

PAGE 100

MAKING DEDUCTIONS

1. Angela

If Angela went to the store at lunch and Bert went at dinner, then Angela went to the store before Bert. While you don't know exactly what time anyone went to the store, lunch is almost always more than two hours before dinner, so Angela must have gone to the store before Karen.

2. Scott

Susan's pet flies, so it can't be a turtle because turtles don't fly. You can't walk a turtle on a leash, so Victor's pet is not a turtle. You do keep pet turtles in a tank. So the only person who can have a turtle is Scott.

3. Bob

We know that Bob ran faster than Evan. If Jim ran slower than Evan, then Bob must have run faster than Jim, too. Since Evan got the silver medal and Bob ran faster, then Bob must have won the gold medal!

4. Tammy

Kim used a spoon to eat her lunch and you don't eat a sandwich with a spoon, so Kim didn't have a sandwich. Since Terry had to use a fork and you don't need a fork to eat a sandwich, then Terry didn't have a sandwich. So only Tammy could have a sandwich and since she brought her lunch in a bag, this seems like a logical deduction!

5. Leslie

Megan's favorite fruit grows on a vine and apples don't grow on a vine. Sara's favorite fruit has seeds on the outside, and apples have seeds on the inside. Since Leslie's favorite fruit grows on a tree and apples grow on a tree, this is the right deduction!

6. John

Tim's favorite sport involves a hoop and there is no hoop in tennis. Mike's favorite sport involves kicking a ball, and no one does that in tennis. So only John is left. Since his favorite sport involves a racquet, then it's just logical that it's John who likes tennis best!

MONDAY

PAGE 103

CROSSWORD

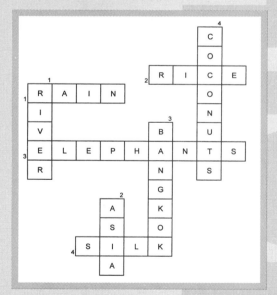

TUESDAY

PAGE 104   ## PAGE 105

MEASURING AREA AND PERIMETER

1. Area: 19   Perimeter: 20
2. Area: 15   Perimeter: 30
3. Area: 25   Perimeter: 32
4. Area: 21   Perimeter: 24
5. Area: 16   Perimeter: 24
6. Area: 25   Perimeter: 28

LOONEY ZOO!

Giraffe Grounds
  Area = 40
  Perimeter = 32

Monkey Mansion
  Area = 26
  Perimeter = 26

Alligator Alley
  Area = 30
  Perimeter = 34

Panda Pad
  Area = 32
  Perimeter = 42

Big Bat Cave
  Area = 44
  Perimeter = 48

Kangaroo Outback
  Area = 32
  Perimeter = 34

Zebra Zone
  Area = 56
  Perimeter = 46

Elephant Heaven
  Area = 32
  Perimeter = 38

WEEK EIGHT

WEDNESDAY

STATE OF AFFAIRS!

Steam – Gas   E
Key – Solid   H
Juice – Liquid   M
Oil – Liquid   I

Oxygen – Gas   U
Doorknob – Solid   L
Guess Who I Am!
HELIUM

THURSDAY

PAGE 108

ROUNDING

1. 600	5. 700	9. 200	13. 700
2. 500	6. 400	10. 600	14. 700
3. 800	7. 300	11. 900	
4. 900	8. 800	12. 700	

PAGE 109

MATH GAMES

3. 16 circles   6. 10 circles
4. 14 circles   7. 8 circles
5. 13 circles

FRIDAY

PAGE 111

ADVERBS

1. quietly
2. there
3. so
4. around
5. out
6. tomorrow

(Possible answers)
7. quickly; slowly
8. upstairs; over
9. yesterday; today
10. quietly; suddenly

SATURDAY

PAGE 112

CRAZY CAPERS

The bank robber is A.

MAZE

PAGE 113

SUBJECT-VERB AGREEMENT

1. ran
2. will go
3. will photograph
4. finished

COMBINE THE SENTENCES

1. Mary, my friend, planted flowers yesterday. OR My friend Mary planted flowers yesterday.
2. Joe, my brother, is really tall. OR My brother Joe is really tall.
3. My Uncle Fred is a policeman. OR Fred, my uncle, is a policeman.
4. Bob, my neighbor, mows his lawn on Sunday. OR My neighbor Bob mows his lawn on Sunday.
5. Frances, my cousin, likes to dance. OR My cousin Frances likes to dance.
6. Jan, Jim's brother, likes dogs. OR Jim's brother Jan likes dogs.
7. Steve, my friend, likes to watch movies. OR My friend Steve likes to watch movies.
8. Dolphins, my favorite animal, live in the ocean. OR My favorite animal, dolphins, live in the ocean.
9. David, my coach's son, plays baseball. OR My coach's son David plays baseball.

CROSSWORD

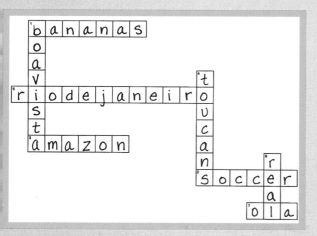

PLACE VALUE

1. 736,238	5. 939,547
2. 194,571	6. 491,521
3. 768,235	7. 356,173
4. 247,128	8. 814,629

NUMBER CRUNCH!

1. 80 + 9 +.5 +.08
2. 800 + 70 + 5
3. 700 + 60 + 5 +.4
4. 1000 + 200 + 60 + 5
5. 900 + 90 + 7 +.2
6. 40 + 5 +.07
7. 800 + 3 +.2
8. 700 + 70 +.05
9. 400 +.2 +.05

MEASURE MAKING!

Cookie sheet – Ruler C
Sugar – Measuring cup B
Butter – Scale A
Flour – Measuring cup S
Chocolate chips – Scale A
Cookies – Ruler U

What am I?
ABACUS

THURSDAY

PAGE 122
NUMBER WORDS

Write each of these numbers in word form.

1. seventy-two thousand, three-hundred and forty-eight
2. thirty-six thousand, six hundred and ninety-two
3. one hundred two thousand, three hundred and fifty-five
4. ninety-eight thousand and six
5. four thousand, nine hundred and eight
6. forty-five thousand, three hundred and twenty-one
7. two hundred twenty thousand and sixty-three
8. twenty-eight thousand, four hundred and fourteen

PAGE 123
MATH GAMES

Add the left and bottom numbers and subtract the number on the right from the sum.

1. 14   2. 24   3. 12
4. 20   5. 23   6. 15

FRIDAY

PAGE 125
ADJECTIVES

1. huge
2. colorful and unusual
3. 5,019.33
4. next week
5. the living room
6. next morning

CHALLENGE

1. 128.72
2. 193.08
3. 16.09

SATURDAY

PAGE 126
FIX THE FACTS

1. A   4. B
2. F   5. D
3. E   6. C

PAGE 127
MAZE

UNSCRAMBLE THE GEOGRAPHY

1. Egypt
2. Brazil
3. United Kingdom
4. Australia
5. China
6. India
7. Italy
8. Thailand

SUNDAY

PAGE 128
FACT VS. OPINION

1. Fact   4. Fact   7. Fact   10. Fact
2. Opinion   5. Opinion   8. Opinion
3. Opinion   6. Fact   9. Opinion

MONDAY
PAGE 131

CROSSWORD

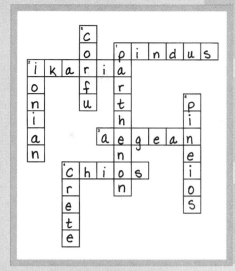

TUESDAY

PAGE 132
MULTIPLICATION AND DIVISION

1. 1,944
2. 71
3. 112
4. 357
5. 3,066
6. 71
7. 1,130
8. 91

PAGE 133
BINGO

1. 48
2. 7
3. 28
4. 64
5. 4
6. 27
7. 24
8. 35
9. 8
10. 9
11. 36
12. 21
13. 2
14. 32
15. 4
16. 56
17. 14
18. 3

Vega won.

WEDNESDAY

PAGE 135
UNLOCK THE ROCK!

Brontosaurus – T

Fern – O

Trilobite – S

Fish – Y

Tyrannosaurus – R

Flat Curled Shell – E

What am I?
OYSTER

THURSDAY

PAGE 136
STORY PROBLEM

1) 1 Hour
2) 5:00 p.m.
3) 5:15 p.m.
4) Yes

PAGE 137
MATH GAMES

1. 35 – Subtract by 5.
2. 54 – Subtract by 6.
3. 74 – Subtract by 8.
4. 48 – Subtract by 7.
5. 31 – Subtract by 6.
6. 36 – Subtract by 8.

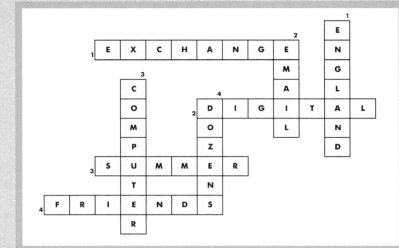

Cat

CROSSWORD

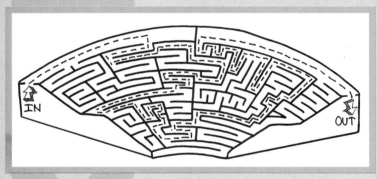

COMPLETE SENTENCES

1. Incomplete   3. Incomplete
2. Complete   4. Complete

1. Equally likely	6. Certain	9. Answers will vary
2. Less likely	7. Answers will vary	10. Answers will vary
3. Impossible	8. Answers will vary	
4. More likely		
5. Certain		

1. 8	4. 5	27 trees
2. 3	5. 2	
3. 8	6. 1	

In Rio de Janeiro and Sydney, the temperatures are colder.
It's warmer in Beijing because it's farther south.

WEEK ELEVEN
THURSDAY

PAGE 150
MATH QUIZ

1. B   4. C
2. A   5. C
3. C   6. A

PAGE 151
MATH GAMES

3. 5 squares
4. 2 squares
5. 3 squares
6. 3 squares
7. 4 squares

FRIDAY

PAGE 153
SEQUENCE OF EVENTS

5, 7, 3, 4, 6, 1, 2, 8

MAZE

SATURDAY

PAGE 154
ADD SOME ADVERBS?

1. carefully, very, today
2. soon, quickly
3. very, quietly, yesterday
4. immediately, extremely, lovely

New answers will vary!

PAGE 155
PREFIXES

1. rewrite
2. misspoke
3. redo
4. prepay

SUNDAY

PAGE 156
ABBREVIATIONS

1. Dr.   7. P.O.
2. Rd.   8. Blvd.
3. St.   9. Sr.
4. U.S.A.   10. Co.
5. Jr.   11. Wed.
6. Sun.   12. Sept.

PAGE 159 READING COMPREHENSION

1. In the Community Center
2. A mural she painted
3. Tripp makes the introduction and gives Mrs. Radanovich a surprise.
4. Mrs. Radanovich's sister
5. Tripp's uncle, a pilot, arranged her flight.
6. Hanging a bulletin board
7. Volunteer of the Month
8. Vega's, Tripp's, and Celeste's
9. They have worked for the good of others and made the neighborhood a better place.

Notes